Copyright @ Ibo Girl, Phina Oruche

All rights reserved. No part of this book may be reproduced, stored or transmitted by any means whether auditory, graphic, mechanical, or electronic without written permission of both publisher and author, except in the case of brief excerpts used in critical articles and reviews. Unauthorized reproduction of any part of this work is illegal and punishable by law.

ISBN 978-4710-8816-2

Liberating Character:

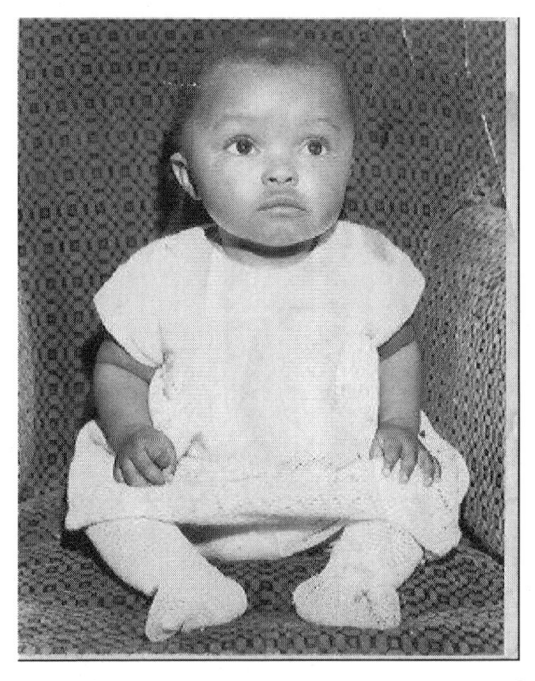

Set the captives free

By Phina Oruche

Thanks for stopping by

Acknowledgements

I am forever indebted to a number of people. Firstly my family of origin, mother, brother and sisters who shaped me, and created the need for me to go and explore. My beautiful and patient husband Stefano, who has held me, consoled me, consistently challenges and walked through triumphs with me, my Italian family, especially Andrea Mariani who painstakingly went through the early drafts as an editor. Elvira de Vico "Il mia Zia Bila" for a cover design that made me cry.
Regina, Roxanna, and the tribe of faith filled women too numerous to mention.
My beautiful son Paolo who lights up my life.

My lovely Chi Chi in heaven who gave me so much love and light in her short life...I thank you.

And the Lord, with me daily through twists and turns.

Contents

Foreword

Chapter One: There's no place like home

Chapter Two: Honour your father and mother

Chapter Three: Sowing the seed

Chapter four: Thick-lipped, ugly bitch

Chapter Five: Run rabbit, run rabbit, run, run, run!

Chapter Six: Say it loud! I am black, and I am proud!

Chapter Seven: All that glitters is not gold

Chapter Eight: Cast me if you can

Chapter Nine: Born to be wild

Chapter Ten: My Redeemer

Chapter Eleven: Finding my family

Chapter Twelve: Famine strikes

Chapter Thirteen: Be careful what you wish for, you might get it

Chapter Fourteen: Truly, Madly, Deeply

Chapter Fifteen: My God shall supply

Chapter Sixteen: Wedding belles

Chapter Seventeen: Honeymoon baby

Chapter Eighteen: Rebirth

Chapter Nineteen: Winds of change

Chapter Twenty: A work in progress

Chapter Twenty-One: Give Him thanks

Foreword or should that say Forward!

"On the day you were born your cord was not cut, nor were you washed with water to make you clean, nor were you rubbed with salt or wrapped in cloths. No one looked on you with pity or had compassion enough to do any of these things for you. Rather, you were thrown out into the open field, for on the day you were born you were despised.

"Then I passed by and saw you kicking about in your blood, and as you lay there in your blood I said to you, 'Live!' I made you grow like a plant of the field. You grew up and developed and became the most beautiful of jewels. Your breasts were formed and your hair grew, you who were naked and bare.

"Later I passed by, and when I looked at you and saw that you were old enough for love, I spread the corner of my garment over you and covered your nakedness. I gave you my solemn oath and entered into a covenant with you, declares the Sovereign Lord, and you became mine.

"You became very beautiful and rose to be a queen. And your fame spread among the nations on account of your beauty, because the splendour I had given you made your beauty perfect, declares the Sovereign Lord."

(Ezekiel 16: 4-14)

Chapter One: There's no place like home

I was almost born into the fire on August 31st 1969. The temperature was red hot and so was the temperament of the environment I landed in. During the final stages of my mother's pregnancy, my father was a very late stage alcoholic and my family had undergone major tragedy.

My beautiful sister had been burnt in a house fire and there was a great deal of Oruche folklore surrounding the incident. I've heard people say it was my father's fault because he was passed out drunk while my siblings placed paper in the grate of a paraffin heater and watched them burn. Rumour has it my older sister dropped the burning paper and accidentally set fire to my middle sister's hideous nylon nightie.

I've also heard that my very heavily pregnant mother sprinted to save my sister's life by extinguishing the flames with her bare hands and that my brother survived the flames by rolling himself up in a mat. I have heard so many things, but I wasn't there so I don't know. All I know is that the scars are real: on the skin of my beautiful sister and on the psyche of my family. I also know that, whatever happened, it didn't end my parent's marriage! Now that's the shocker for me.

The human spirit is amazing. My mother can be a spiritual giant, a towering inferno and, coexisting in the same vessel, a weak, victimised woman. At that time, she was a young, disappointed bride. She had come to England from Nigeria seeking a better life. Her older, brilliant husband was a shoo-in for Cambridge; he had come from excellent stock. He came from a family of bishops and clergymen if folklore is to be believed.

My mother can be quite liberal with the truth; for example, she claims she narrowly missed being the first Nigerian supermodel and tennis champion, though there are no records of this so I can never be sure. According to my mum, my father had taken the villagers' financial pledges of support, but never quite made it to university, sidelined as he was by an extraordinary gene: the alcoholic gene. My mother had been bruised and crushed by his alcoholism to the point at which she found herself weak and trapped in Liverpool rather than Cambridge; a little off track there! Excessive alcohol can do that to you.

My father, according to my mother's account, swindled her and her mother's inheritance from my grandfather. It's a very cloudy account, but it speaks of trust being broken. Apparently, a significant amount of money was left to my mother by her father, but because of my grandmother's age and illiteracy, the menfolk were sent to claim this money on her behalf.

A trusted older male relative and my very young, sheltered and naive mother – who was a teenager at that time – went along as family representatives. Somehow my father, who was twenty years older than my mother, was also in the little collection party. It's not clear whether he was a friend of the older relative or how he came to be there, but it was decided that the best use of this inheritance money was to purchase a taxi. It wasn't a fortune, so they suggested it would be best used to buy something that would generate income. Somehow my father managed to get a taxi on hire purchase, unbeknown to my ancestral family, and by the time they found out he had ripped them off (when the taxi was repossessed), it was too late.

OK, so if that's a truthful account of things it's pretty awful. My mother maintains that she was hugely saddened by what happened and the effect it had on her grieving mother. So she decided she would heal the hurt by getting the money back from this swindler. But then she claims that he used black magic on her and that at some point she got married to him without her own knowledge or consent. What?!

This is more than my mind can take. I wonder whether it's a difference in culture; as much as I want to be an African female, I am completely baffled by any notion of this type of African Ju-Ju. But my mother is adamant and sticks to her story to this day. She says she felt powerless; as though she had let the family down badly. It's a small village and she felt everyone was judging her, so she went off and married the very same man and moved with him to England, where she kept asking him for the money back! It doesn't make sense to me at all, but she maintains that it's all true.

Naturally having more experience and acumen, he outfoxed her at every turn, but because he was a wonderful businessman they started a life and a family together. He was unpredictable, though, and liked the drink too much. She naively asked him to stop but he couldn't or wouldn't and there she was, far from family, the prodigal daughter: unable or unwilling to go back.

She found herself in a very violent, unhealthy marriage with an untrustworthy alcoholic who kept letting her down. His businesses were falling apart because the alcohol had wrecked his focus and his ability to do the things he needed to do to maintain his success.

A marriage that started in deceit was floundering in infidelity. Women were coming and going, and one of them was a married friend of the family. Amid dysfunction that beggars belief we, as children, saw a lot of patrol cars and strange behaviour. My father was often locked up overnight and told to sober up. As my mother got more and more frustrated, she started to demand change and tried to remove herself and us from the situation, but he responded with beatings. My sister has told me about violence that I fortunately don't remember or didn't witness.

My mother tried to get help from 'friends', but they weren't interested in getting involved because he wouldn't go away quietly. If you got in the line of fire he would break your door down and smash your face in until you returned his wife and kids to him. She quickly learnt that – as women in situations of domestic abuse often learn (especially in the early seventies) – violence was considered to be an issue for married couples to deal with; the police were reluctant to get involved.

The other thing was that alcoholics often get entangled with the police, and there was concern over what would happen to him if she called the cops. He was on various warnings and bonds, so even though he had caused her more than a decade of torture and pain, she couldn't bring herself to destroy him entirely. I'm not sure what I make of all this, but it's the backdrop to my story.

Trapped in this awful predicament, my mother finally had the courage to start the painful process of leaving when I was three. Apparently, I was found drunk in the street at this point and had to be rushed to the hospital to have my stomach pumped! Now this ticks me off, but it underscores a prevalent theme in my household: neglect, denial and bad behaviour.

Question: how can a three-year-old drink liquor, isn't it an acquired taste? How did I get it and why wasn't someone caring for me? This doesn't quite do it for me. Where were the lovely pink walls to my nursery; the handed down teddy that once belonged to my grandma; the lovely bedtime stories; the princesses and fairies of childhood? Where was the tooth fairy? All this was nonexistent for me.

I didn't come through that passage of delight and many children don't, but if it doesn't kill you it will make you stronger. Truthfully, the families that live under the vile threatening cycle of any addiction are way too busy fixing the addict, and the spouse is usually taken up with surviving and repairing the damage. Don't get me wrong, I was loved fiercely; suffocated with physical love actually, and I still am. But I was criminally neglected. We all were. And there were obstacles to climb before I could even dare to dream. I had to climb out of that house first, out of the ghetto, out of the broken home lined with disappointment and abandonment before I could gain the tools to be all that I was created to be.

There are four of us kids and I am the youngest. I have two older sisters and an older brother; there are six years between us all. My mother started young and was married and divorced young. This was a time when divorce was not common, and there was an element of shame to it. It was hard for her to make friends because women were worried that she, a natural beauty, would attract the eyes of their husbands. Now that's both sad and hilarious; my beautiful mother was so beaten and wretched she wasn't interested in getting her hands on any man.

My earliest memory is of us in our house in Halewood on the outskirts of Liverpool. We must have moved there just after my mother and father divorced. He was eventually deported after she did what she feared most: she got the courts and police involved at the highest level.

Divorce does many things, and one of them is that it rips the family's finances apart. We were not the richest of families, so my mum would have us chase one another around the streets whenever we were fortunate enough to have a new outfit. It seems crazy, but I remember as kids being instructed to show off our new clothes. And to me that shows how poor we were. My mother still wants us to look like we have it going on; no matter what's going on behind closed doors she wants us to appear fine. But we didn't feel poor. We were clean, we were strong and we were loved.

My mother's niece, my first cousin, came to live with us at one point. Apparently, she had had a battle with my father because, according to my mother, he had tried to rape her some time before in Nigeria. My lovely cousin is significantly older than me, so I looked up to her. I still to this day call her aunty, though technically she's my cousin. My mother has one sister who is so much older than her that her first child is more like my mother's sister than her own sister is. They used to go out in identical platform shoes, wigs and boob tubes. You can only imagine the mess two young Nigerian women could get into looking like that in Liverpool during the seventies. But that was my background: strong, wild, vibrant women.

I'm grateful for that, but every coin has two sides. For all her vibrancy and strength, my mother was literally a law unto herself. She had no one to answer to, but she also had no one to lean on when times were tough, as they often were. So ultimately she had no one to help her. Personally, I think she cracked under the strain.

My mother told me one day she was coming down the stairs and saw me taking a dining room chair and half carrying, half dragging it to the front door. Now I must have been three-and-a-half years old at this point. She watched in horror as my father taught me how to open the front door to let him in. I loved my dad, apparently.

What's really strange is that I honestly, hand on heart, have no recollection of him or of this incident, or of the many other violent incidents that were relayed to me later on. All I have is a photo of him with his brothers in Nigeria in the fifties wearing Bermuda shorts with a shirt and tie. My father has his mouth wide open and a grin on his face. He looks like a raconteur; that's a quality I have and the smile is reminiscent of the one I see on myself when I tell stories, and on the faces of my siblings.

I have one picture of my father, it should be worn out the amount of times I've looked at it. Because I was born on his birthday I am called "Adannaya", which means "father's daughter" in Ibo, one of the major languages spoken in Nigeria. But he has become a truly silent character in my life. Apparently, he came to the house and took my brother and sister after the divorce. Some say he was driving them to an airport in London, others to a ship in Liverpool, but whatever the vessel, the destination was always the same: they were Nigeria bound. I hate this story because it makes me feel like he didn't choose me. Whether this is true or not, there was an injunction that prevented him from gaining access to us at this point. The idea that he used my love for him to potentially get in the house certainly fits the selfish profile of an alcoholic, who naturally does whatever he or she needs to do to stay fixed. So my mother decided to put us in a place where he couldn't get to us. After all he had, through his drinking, allowed himself to be removed from our lives by forever scarring his daughter; passing out and allowing her to end up with third-degree burns on ninety percent of her face and body when he should have been caring for her.

My mother was able to get anything done; a superwoman, that's what I remember. At one point she was studying for a degree, bringing up four kids and raising her own kind of hell! She would resolutely help anyone in her bloodline, from her sisters to her own children. She is still like that; adversity has done nothing to abate that giving spirit in her.

She did whatever she needed to do to get the job done and still does now. At one point we packed up and moved to Runcorn, a small subsidiary about 30 miles outside Liverpool. She was excited because she had managed to get her four children a brand new, never-before-lived-in council house. She had used her misfortune to the fullest. It was a detached semi with four bedrooms; a veritable luxury for her and for us. I shared a bedroom with my middle sister, while my mum, my brother and my oldest sister had rooms of their own. Our room was typical seventies. There were two single beds, woodchip wallpaper that had been painted lilac and a really rough yellow carpet with a burn on it. The carpet was obviously a remnant because it didn't reach the walls on any side, so we had wooden floorboards before they were trendy (although ours weren't varnished. They were stained alright, but not in the conventional sense). We had white nets and blue-and-violet-flowered nylon curtains.

Our window looked out over the garden, and what we called the 'first woods'. There was a bus route that divided these woods and an underground tunnel through a stream that we used to crawl through as a rite of passage to a place we called the 'second woods'.

We also had a fairly wobbly teak (think chipboard) wardrobe from MFI that my poor mother must have assembled. This is the seventies, honey, so there was no IKEA. We had an old wooden gramophone casing that someone had thrown out, which we used as a sort of vanity/bookcase.

I also had a picture of Michael Jackson (may God rest his soul) from the period just after his spilt with the Jackson Five. I was sure I would marry Michael one day. I had so many old Jackson Five albums and singles and knew every word of every single top ten-hit. Top of the Pops stars The Specials, Madness and Bananarama were also among my favourites. But some of my musical tastes, such as Northern Soul, were gleaned from my siblings.

But I didn't really fit in with the others because very early on I was deemed the baby, which I hated! During this time our family unit was tiny. There was no dad on the scene and no more cousins, because even though we had an abundance of them we couldn't ever afford to meet up. I never imagined I would get on a plane in my life.

I went to a small primary school that was within walking distance of the house. I remember everything being muddy because the development was barely finished; in fact, when I started at that school it was still meeting in prefabricated mobiles. On my first day at school I sat at a wooden double desk with little inkwell holes and no one sitting on the other side. I was the only black person in the room. This was wonderful training for the entertainment industry, as often I am the only black person in a cast, though things are getting better.

The next day a little girl came and sat next to me and everybody made fun of her, but I didn't realise it was because she was sitting next to the 'blackie'. The kids used racial slurs against me, but their ignorance showed because they would sing: "Chinese, Japanese don't forget to wash your knees". It used to really hurt, but now I think it's funny, because I clearly don't look Japanese!

That little girl, Lorri is still one of my greatest friends to this day and she figures extensively in my story, often acting as a catalyst. I don't see her as often as I used to because we live in different parts of the world, but we recently talked and got our children together and it was a gorgeous, glorious day. Lorri tells me she only realised I was black when we were about eleven, five or so years after we first met, because although she had heard rumours from others, that's when Diana Ross broke through. This proves the fact that racism is learned, because as five-year-old girls we didn't know anything about it.

I was very shy about anything relating to faith. My mother was very devout when we were children, because after what she had been through she had to be. She used to sit us around the living room on a Sunday and make us read the scriptures while we took the mickey.

My siblings and I were generally a bunch of mickey takers. Being so different from our peers we were used to cracking jokes and coming on with the funnies as a survival mechanism. So my mother would sit us in a circle with our little Good News Bibles. We would guffaw and scream and nearly wet our pants laughing, refusing to take it seriously. We would fall on the floor and feign sleep, pretend to slit our wrists and play dead; anything apart from what we were supposed to do. She had to sweat and struggle to discipline us because it was not cool to read the Bible. Imagine me, the youngest, at my worst and then multiply that by four. Then think of my poor mother… we really were naughty kids.

My mother made it her business to watch the daily news every day, on the hour. It seems excessive, but she had no balance, no friends, no family and no life apart from us. She had been left with four children, with no discernible means of support; either financially, emotionally or spiritually. She had no physical male affection; no hugs, no kisses. She devoted her life to serving us. She was very sacrificial that way and she paid the price for it with her sanity.

Having said that, she became very adept at getting what she wanted. But while I applaud the end results, back then the means were usually horrific and loaded with negative consequences.

Chapter Two: Honour your father and mother

So, as I said, I come from a place where men were alcoholics and dope fiends. They were violent and unpredictable. You could spend your life giving birth to their children and mopping up their messes with the law, only for them to ultimately betray you with another woman or, worse, beat you up in front of your children and make you feel like death. Many women were groomed to tolerate a lot of nonsense, but to everyone else the men seemed absolutely charming; I know that sounds impossible, but they did.

I was bullied, beaten up and humiliated at home by my brother, but I fought it every step of the way. I love my brother with all my heart, but he was my adversary growing up, my biggest tormentor. I have a real soft spot for him now, but he was the one that created the tape that used to play in my mind; his voice taunted me, calling me "a thick-lipped, ugly bitch". He would spit in my dinner, slam doors in my face and just constantly hate, bully and degrade me.

Once, I brought a friend home. As I walked through the door, he came down the stairs as calm as you like and slapped me clean across the face, knocking me down. I got straight up, ran upstairs sobbing and never came back down. I wanted to die and just couldn't face my friend. In the outside world I was popular, had a great sense of humour, a lot of levity, and was nutty; probably induced by the freedom I lacked at home.

To the outsider my brother was quite charming; he laughed and joked with people. At home he was sullen, brooding, violent, and unpleasant, just like his father before him. He acted out precisely what he had seen in him and went out of his way to belittle me. We would have the usual kid-on-kid altercations about bathroom rights and other petty things before I left for school, but he had an incredible memory and no matter how long I was at school and after-school programmes, I would eventually have to come home.

So what do you say to someone when your home life is like that, when you just want to shrivel up and die? Perhaps that's why I brought my friend home in the first place, as protection, because he was normally very concerned with people's opinions of him. Somehow I started to imagine that it was my fault, that I didn't deserve respect, and that he was treating me like the rubbish I was.

When I was younger I decided that was never going to happen to me again, anywhere else, ever. I would never again be controlled by a man, by kids or by a lack of money. Initially my plan was simple, I would just run from the scene of the crime; as far away as I could. I would survive by living in denial about how bad it had been, or how badly I was affected by it.

My mother didn't protect me from my brother, correct him or help either of us, numbed as she was by the ten years of brutality she had suffered during her abusive marriage. My older sister remembers my mother's head bouncing off every step in the house at the hands of my father, but I can't remember anything about him. I realise as I research more and ask more questions, I developed this selective memory for my own protection.

My mother often told me she was saving up to leave him and that she had stashed the money in a pair of boots. Then one night my father brought a woman home from his previous night's bender, something I can't imagine any man doing to me. My mother was devastated, but not because the woman was there. She was destroyed by the fact that, when the woman left, she wore my mother's boots, taking the getaway money with her. Imagine living like that! I can't, but in a way I did because my brother mimicked nearly everything he saw his father do and did it to me.

Aged twelve or so I felt that I didn't fit anywhere as we were the only black children in our school and I was getting bullied at home. I always wore a big smile, so everyone always assumed I was alright. I wasn't!

The scenario at home was useful in its own way. Seeds were being sown in my youth for me to want to be the biggest, baddest, strongest thing I could be, so that I could be safe. My ambition was born out of a desperate need.

Initially I wanted to be a star because it seemed that if you were a star you had no problems. I know now that this is utter nonsense. My friend's daughter, who is eleven, wants to be a celebrity. I asked what she wanted to be famous for and she was shocked; she didn't realise celebrity used to be about being known for your art or showbiz talent. It was never about going into the jungle (more on that later) and eating bugs, or marrying a millionaire, or living in a house with cameras following your dull life twenty-four hours a day.

All she sees is the shallowness: the limousines and the magazines. She's too young to understand it's not a cure-all. If you have issues before you hit the big time the pressures will be there to eat you alive. People demand your time and talent, they want you to help them promote their projects, clothes and agendas, and if you don't know who you are, it can shake you apart. I was like that eleven-year-old girl. I wanted to impress and be insulated by money, fortune and fame; in a word, to be 'untouchable'. I chose acting because I wanted to be something else, someone else; anything but me.

On my first day of secondary school I met a light-skinned youth of about fourteen, think Phil Lynott with his big afro. I was charmed to see him, because this was the first time I had seen a person of colour, who wasn't related to me, in a school setting. During the first break I scanned the playground to look for him but couldn't see him. I wondered where he was, but didn't get a chance to dwell on it because there was a group of kids in a circle that alerted everyone to the fact a fight was taking place inside. I crept through the circle, transfixed and with fear in my heart. I already knew what I would see and my fears were realised when I saw the mixed-race boy on the ground having been repeatedly hit on the head with a brick. I was saddened but not entirely shocked. He came back to school that afternoon with part of his hair shaved and a bandage on his head; I don't recall ever seeing him again.

It took a long time to find acceptance and balance in Runcorn, but I finally began to come into my own. I had some good friends; hard won, but good. I managed to outlive the legacy of my middle sister who had a fearsome reputation, though I'll defend her to my death. You try having third-degree burns, growing up as the only Nigerian at your school and being the only person from a divorced family, with no father on the scene. Imagine people asking questions about your hair and your skin, about where your dad is.

My mother didn't help matters. She was loud, embarrassing and caused trouble, either coming to school in miniskirts or full Nigerian attire, complete with headdress. I love all that now, and have spent a great deal of time on the African continent. Nigeria is a wonderful country with an amazing accent that makes me smile, but back then people tried to shame us by claiming they couldn't understand a word she was saying, so we always had a lot of explaining to do.

Then add my brother to the mix. Having been expelled from my school, he left behind him a fierce reputation, which in street cred terms is your calling card. Then there was a music teacher, let's call him Mr Barker, who hated my brother wholeheartedly. I don't know what my brother did to aggravate him but the idea of his little sister being in the class allowed Mr Barker to exhibit vile racism and revenge. He wouldn't have dared speak that way to my fearsome brother, so he did it to a little girl instead! He used to sing slave songs and Negro spirituals to humiliate me. He asked me to sing "Jump down, turn around, pick a bale of cotton. Jump down, turn around, pick a bale a day" with him in front of the class, assuming in his racial insanity that I would know the words. How could I possibly know the words when I had barely left Liverpool all my life?

But that was the least of my problems; my home life was still a nightmare. Because of his alcoholic father, his frightened and emotionally unstable mother, the pedestal he was put on and the prominence he was given, my poor brother was built up and then dropped from a great height, as I was. Being abandoned by your father is hard for anyone, but especially for a little boy who had been so spoilt and cherished. Who does he turn to? I believe he had a hard time getting over it. I believe the pain he felt manifested itself in his need to make the only thing smaller than him in the house feel worthless. It seems he had a kind of 'kick-the-dog' syndrome, only in this case I was the dog!

My brother was cruel. He contradicted every word I said, very seldom allowed me to speak and kicked me down the stairs. I was told repeatedly that no one would ever love me. Whenever I went to one of the two toilets we had in the old house he would decide he also wanted to go and would reach in and would drag me off, often midway through whatever I was doing.

He wouldn't allow me to watch TV and his favourite cruel trick was to lie in front of it holding up a newspaper so that I couldn't see the screen. If I changed the channel he would start screaming, claiming he was watching it. I learned so many tricks from having to deal with him, one of which was to complain about a show I liked so he would keep it on, or laugh at one I didn't like so he would immediately turn it over. I would have to make occasional complaints about my favourite programmes so he would leave them on.

I don't know whether this was a normal level of sibling rivalry because I've never lived in another household or shared another family's dirty laundry. But it felt excessive to me. I used to alternate between wanting to kill myself and wanting him dead. I used to plot his assassination and, in my childlike ways, do things like pouring water into his beloved stereo hoping that when he got home from school and turned it on it would go "boom" and explode, like it would have done in a cartoon. Wile E Coyote was my master teacher in this, but he let me down!

I was raised in a brutal fight for my own survival. I was schooled to think that it was a dog-eat-dog world; to strike first before someone strikes you. What a legacy, what a mess! But it's nice to know you can heal from it, and be assured you can. My ambition was born out of trying to prove to him and my often negligent mother that I was worth loving, that I was worth protecting.

As a little girl I wanted an ally, a playmate, a brother and a friend. I love him fiercely: even now blood is thicker than water. I forgive him for all that stuff, as I want to be free to love and succeed in life. I recently had him walk me down the aisle at my wedding, but it's still one step forward and two back. I mention this not to embarrass him, but to outline what shaped me and made me the way I am today. To expose the raw material God had to work with.

I want the best for him, but he is not of this world somehow. As we got older, I understood that his issues weren't with me. This super-intelligent boy and I were competing for my distracted mother's attention. We were competing because we were living in a single parent family, with four kids and a mother who was '419 scamming' (Nigerian slang for intellectual fraud). She was studying, doing work experience, experiencing discrimination and battling the frustrations of not being able to make her very superior, hard-won education count.

She was trying to be everything to everybody, but there wasn't enough of her to go round. My brother had his heart broken by our drunken father before dad lurched off into obscurity, as we all did. He had that African spirit, that male-dominated ideal. It took me a long time to stop fighting that, but I have made my peace with it in some ways, because it's either that or a weak man, and I can't bear weak men.

I have the proudest mother in the world. Exodus 20:12 says: "Honour your father and your mother, so that you may live long in the land the Lord your God is giving you." It so clearly states that this is what I am supposed to do, but I have a hard time doing it. There is so much water under the bridge that I have forgiven but it often rises again, threatening to drown me with each new incident.

Truthfully, I love her, but she is overbearing. She is capable of such endearing sweetness, but would smother me if I allowed her to. Her favouritism towards me made my life very uncomfortable with the others as a kid as she inadvertently set me up as the outsider. My mother has always been very proud of my accomplishments and I, in turn, was churning them out as fast as I could to try and get the praise, love and self-esteem I so badly wanted. The fact that my mother's fears actually prevented us from meeting our goals meant the whole scenario was utter madness.

As a case in point, I had been selected as a gymnast to do pre-trials for the Junior Olympics, but my mother wouldn't let me go. So, after being asked to model in a fashion show when I was fourteen on a school trip to Spain, I seized the opportunity. My battered soul and self-esteem thought: 'Yes, maybe I have a chance, a way out of abuse, sadness and being told by default that there is no future for me'. If that's what you are currently hearing, I tell you it's a lie! You can be whatever you dream if you work hard at it and take no shortcuts.

I remember telling a teacher in Aigburth Vale what I wanted to do academically, but even though I was studying chemistry, biology and Art A-Levels, she advised me to become a cleaner. So whatever you feel about yourself in your soul, hold onto it, even if it seems ridiculous to everyone else: including your teachers.

At first, when I was asked to model I was horrified, but I was up to my eyeballs in detention so I negotiated doing it in order to get out of trouble. Naturally I loved it and I knew I wanted to pursue this as an avenue out of the ghetto. All around me in Toxteth, girls were getting pregnant to boys who couldn't father the children that came. By the time the kids were born, the boys had moved onto other girls who were 'fresh', who didn't have any 'baggage'. They didn't realise this baggage was their offspring, their future, their legacy. It was a terrible time.

Chapter Three: Sowing the seed

When I was fifteen, we ended up back in Liverpool. During the day I went to school, but it was difficult because I was the only newbie. Like all Nigerian parents, my mother went on and on about getting great 'O-Level' results so I could make it to university. Then, right in the middle of my exam year, she did a moonlight flit because she owed all kinds of money and was in fear, poor love.

I was the new girl in a new school, which taught the two-year curriculum the opposite way from the way I had learned it. It was decided that I would sit in the library and study the new stuff on my own but who, at fifteen, has that kind of discipline? I certainly didn't. Subsequently I didn't mesh with the other already cliqued pupils.

At home we went from four bedrooms to two. The house was actually supposed to be for my two sisters to live in. My oldest sister, then nineteen, had given up her flat to save money for the move, so she was living with us temporarily. Fortunately, my middle sister hadn't left her flat yet, as it turned out my mum's desperate action crushed my older sister's spirit right out of her body.

She went from the exciting independence of getting her first property to being forced back into childhood, into the house where she had had a difficult time with my mother. She had lived far from home since she was a very young teenager and she found herself in a real slump: staying in bed, chain smoking cigarettes and sharing a room with her fifteen-year-old sister and mother, while her brother – anger on legs – freaked out in the bedroom next door. Unsurprisingly, I didn't do as well as I could have in my exams! And the cherry on the cake was my brother opening the results envelope when it came and using its contents to humiliate me.

I needed help badly and I found it in the form of a wonderful teenage friend in Liverpool. She saved my derriere, because outside that madhouse I had someone who cared. DS was two years older than me, and she was the youngest of a tribe of children: two girls and lots of boys. She was cheeky and hilarious – a complete crack-up – and her house, though fun, was a much-needed safe haven for me.

She had a very strong sense of self and didn't let her older brothers bully her, which was incredible from where I stood. She was very stylish in that 1980s way; think Madonna circa 1985 with a tint and a perm! She told me about matching colours and never wearing more than three, ever. I obeyed the 'rules' studiously because I was desperate to belong.

It was DS I brought home the day my brother knocked me down. I had shared everything with her except my secret shame: the torture I was experiencing at home. I just didn't want her to see that; I was playing at being normal. I didn't bother reporting him to my mother, she had her own problems, and I avoided DS for days. When I could face her again we carried on like nothing had happened. Come on, what would I say? What, as a seventeen-year-old girl, could she have done, or proposed? Ignoring it was the only way forward then. I could and would smile through anything.

During my time in Toxteth I had a revelation about all things black. That's when my black pride kicked it. My childhood was spent trying to fit into an all-white Runcorn, trying to downplay my Nigerian roots and play up being Scouse; to assimilate rather than drawing attention to myself. But after DS and Toxteth combined I changed my mind on that one. I found my first creative outlet: clothes! All week was spent getting my clothes ready for Saturday night; going into town and dancing in Saturdays or Kirklands; blagging drinks from men and then running away before heading to the afterhours dive we called 'The Blues'. These were some of the funniest times in my life. No one knows how to party like people who have nothing to lose. Often I go to an event now and am bored to tears as everyone is just trying to network and be somebody. Whatever happened to just having a good old dance?!

Those fashion lessons, night-time parties, being able to get myself together and find someone who cared enough to spend time with me was like medicine to my battered soul. After school I would get together with DS and her friends and we would plan for Friday and Saturday nights and talk nonsense about boys.

No one messed with either of us; probably because she had so many brothers. Well not the boys our age anyway. We used to sit in her fifteen-year-old friend's boyfriend's house. He was a Rasta and was twice her age. The old Rastas didn't care that they had nothing to offer us in terms of respect, fidelity and commitment. They would smoke spliffs, which I tried it once and, to my embarrassment, spent the rest of the evening on the bathroom floor hugging the toilet. They would letch after us and DS and I would giggle to each other and say: "Yeah, right… as if".

During the day I would have to walk past all the Rastas we saw at night in my school uniform. They heckled and shouted "African Queen" at me. All of a sudden I was considered good looking, and after all I had been told as a child, I quite liked it. But at night we would just take their drinks, flirt and disappear.

I got into Jamaican culture big time. We were shunned by the Nigerian contingent because my mother didn't want us to speak that way, but the street dictated that all things Jamaican were cool so we were all desperate to fit in and got our little patois accents down pat. One of the girls I knew at the time asked me why I bothered with school seeing as it was a "white man's qualification". I said: "Well it's a white man's country, so it might help." I later found out the girl became a prostitute, so thank God I preferred my education.

The strange thing is, this should have been an incredibly awful time. In a lot of ways it was, but I guess I also have a strong spirit crafted by adversity because, believe it or not, it was also a lot of fun. Although it felt like it would lead nowhere and I was desperate to escape it, I still remember that period with fondness.

People always ask me why I went to the States so young. I was running as hard and fast as I could from the nightmare I was raised in.

There was a pattern that was too painful for me to see, never mind cope with. I finally told my mother I couldn't cope with her incessant changeability. She's brilliant, but living with her can be so turbulent. So America it was; a fresh start, somewhere I hoped I would not be bound by the colour of my skin.

But I had a practice run in London first. All small-town kids want to go to the capital. I had been to the Notting Hill Carnival and Madame Tussaud's with DS. Just being in London was the thrill of a lifetime and being next to anyone famous, even a waxwork dummy, appealed to me. I was desperate to rise above the humble beginnings that so often horrified me.

Fate has its way of moving you. I probably wouldn't ever have set foot in London on my own, but my mother had left me, following in the footsteps of her daughters and moving to London to search for work. Fair enough, she had been waiting and searching for work my whole life and had experienced many years of rejection. She needed the income and the breath of fresh air that a life outside her previous existence would bring.

I encouraged her because she used to cry all the time; she had studied a lot and still couldn't find a job. I wanted her to have the life she deserved, but because I looked out for her I was left alone with the brother who terrified me. This forced me to make a decision. I used to secretly take the train up to Manchester for a modelling course. How ridiculous, there is no such thing as modelling school, but I was naïve, so what did I know? I now know you learn on the job, but there are always people at the fringes of the entertainment and fashion industry who are waiting to capitalise on your need. I 'graduated' modelling school in a hurry so I could get to safety. The next day I got up and left for London. My only regret was that in my haste I never got a chance to say goodbye to DS, and I've saw her since until recently the wonders of facebook.

Getting up and starting a new life without so much as a goodbye to the old one or anyone in it has been a recurrent theme in my life. I had the best teacher in the world when it came to that.

Even though I had two sisters and a mother living there, I was on my own when I got to London. I stayed with two men I knew from Liverpool for a while and had a big crush on their older brother. But one day I left through the bathroom window when one of the brothers kept trying to run his hands over my body. To this day he reckons he was joking, but I wasn't so sure. I asked my mum and sisters if I could live with them, but the "no" was deafening and hurt quite a bit. I ended up getting a job as a night-time telephonist at The Grosvenor Hotel so I could have my days free as a potential model. Fortunately, the job came with a room.

This was a time of tremendous rejection. It seemed as though my family didn't want me and neither did the industry. My mother decided to help me by coaching me on what to say to get a council flat and, after a while, it worked. I got fired from my job for sleeping during the shift, which was fair enough. But I was off to my new flat so I didn't need the room any more.

I used to think modelling was about girls leaning on cars, a residual thought from the sexist shots of girls on motors that dominated the seventies while I was growing up. I always pretended I was joking, but I was deadly serious about wanting to get out of the mess I was in. Having said that, I was smart enough to know that no one would support my dream, so I didn't tell anyone I had one.

I was only fourteen but masquerading as eighteen, so of course I got myself into endless scrapes that I didn't have the experience for. I was desperately trying to be somebody and was exuding confidence that I didn't have. We call it 'fake it till you make it'! I wanted to take the fashion world by storm but, judging by my first pictures, you have to laugh at my bravery.

Chapter four: Thick-lipped, ugly bitch

London's modelling scene in the nineties was really exciting for me; I was so obsessed with the top models. I had a nasty flat in a tower block off the Old Kent road and I was on the top floor. The lift had urine in it and the back stairs had been used by lazy tenants to dispose of months and months of garbage. I was instructed by my mother to lie and I say I was pregnant in order to get the flat, and the lovely council did what they did to all young, pregnant girls: they put me in a ghetto they thought I would never escape. Wrong!

I'm ashamed to admit my mother and I later had a fist fight as she tried to take over and move in. She was already causing havoc living with my older sister and there was no way on earth I was going to let her take a strike at my independence. I had very little to keep me going at that time and my little flat with one bin bag of belongings and a stained mattress were not going to stop me or put out the pilot light in my heart; the light that spurred on my being selected to model in Spain; the spark that believed that I could be one of them, that I could do it too.

I decided to go and work for Storm modelling agency. I was the book girl and Girl Friday. Kate Moss, a scruffy, short girl from Croydon, came in with her one passport-sized photo in her portfolio. I didn't think she would ever catch on; that shows just how much I knew! There were also the goddesses whose books I sent out with longing, but who would show up at the agency looking so bland and ordinary. I started to understand that it was about bone structure, posture and height; that most of the girls didn't look like much in the natural, but the army of make-up artists, stylists and hairdressers made all the difference in the world.

Fashion magazines meant so much to me. It was a chance to live a different way and I ended up pasting pictures of the girls all over the walls of my dodgy flat. They were all over the hallway, and not in an average teenager kind of way. I'm talking obsessive compulsive; there wasn't a square inch that wasn't covered with Naomi Campbell,

Gail O'Neill, Gail Elliott, Yasmin Le Bon, Cindy Crawford, Christy Turlington and Akure Wall. Then I also had Nelson Mandela, who had, I think, just been released from jail. Keeping him company were Spike Lee, who had burst onto the scene as a film maker; Maya Angelou, whose voice is invaluable to any young girl trying to make it out of a bad situation; and of course Bill Cosby, Lisa Bonet and Kadeem Hardison from A Different World, a spinoff from The Cosby Show. I didn't know then, but that mad collage became like a compass. I met, worked with or became friends with nearly all of these people when I moved to New York and later Los Angeles. But they were a million miles from me at this point.

Like all models I walked around London, hopping on and off the tube to castings and 'go-sees' (so called because you had to 'go see' such and such). My first rounds of pictures were absolutely ridiculous. Suffice to say I had on purple lipstick. Me, with the size of my mouth! My hair was badly straightened so all five of my hairs looked ridiculous; I looked more like a Nigerian student than a model. I also had a lazy eye muscle so, although you couldn't tell in person, my left eye looked much smaller than my right in photos.

Sophistication came to me slowly. One time my sisters invited me to lunch in Victoria as one of them worked there. I remember it being a big deal going into Victoria with my sisters because they usually clubbed together as the older, wiser two and I was a little kid to them. I arrived in cut-off denim shorts, grey woolly tights and a long mannish coat! Think boy in drag! I'd had a perm, which I think was called 'leisure curl', but it was one small step up from a wet look.

My sisters told me that if I was serious about this modelling lark I needed to pay more attention to my fashion sense and appearance. I was outraged! I was so angry with them at the time and remember thinking they hated me and wanted to spoil things for me. In reality, a simple "thank you" would have sufficed. Now, in hindsight, I'm very grateful. I think youth, or desperation, protects you from a lot.

I am not too proud to admit I had no bloody clue about London, fashion or 'the scene', but what I didn't know I made up for in drive and determination. It was a nightmare to break into the business at first. Naomi Campbell was 'IT', the only one people wanted. There were lots of other black models knocking around at the time, but it seemed as though the agencies would only take on one at a any given time. I remember going around and being told "we already have a black girl". Competition was fierce.

Ironically, after I came back to shoot Footballers' Wives in 2005 – fourteen years later – I was still being told the same thing. People were just a bit more polite about it because of the success I had had. It amazed me that with a major series under my belt, racism still continued unabated in the UK. Americans are all about what sells, so if you sell, you sell. They don't care where you come from or what colour you are. I entered The Clothes Show competition at one point in a desperate attempt to break in. Although I was too short for their requirements at just under five foot eight, I ended up on a TV newsreel, which was exciting. I got noticed and it spurred me on.

After being sent away by all the agencies in London more than once (including Storm, who I worked for), an agency finally took me on. The agency was called Nevs, and after the first week they sent me to Kenya to shoot a Guinness commercial. Wow! I got a crash course in excess and fabulousness, primarily because I was out there for a week but only actually worked for about four hours. I was put up in a swanky hotel and given daily pocket money; I was hooked!

Tramping the streets of London in all weathers wasn't brilliant, but the results were amazing, and of course I met an army of young models every day. I had a laugh with these girls, most of whom were working class girls like me and were using their 'beauty', determination or desperation to move from one level, where they were living on hope, to an entirely different one.

I was lining up with my destiny because the majority of my modelling career played out on TV. I did editorial too, but I mostly did ads, especially in London. Tony Kaye of Tony Kaye films was amazing to me; he put me in commercial after commercial. And a few years later, when I moved to Los Angeles, he paid the 900 dollars I had to come up with to get started in the Screen Actors Guild. You can't make a move in the States without it, so I can't put into words the gratitude I have towards that man.

I remember he had one bit of advice for me: "Never lose your Scouse accent". I was very nervous about my intellect, and always felt conscious of my Liverpudlian accent. People always copy a Scouse accent, repeating the way you say things rather than listening to what you're actually trying to say. It can make you really nervous and I didn't realise until later that it was a compliment and a blessing that the Scouse voice is so mimicked. Tony celebrated my voice and thought I was really funny. So I must apologise to him now. "Sorry Tone, it's battered!" That's what happens after years of playing American characters on American TV shows. But slowly and surely it's re-emerging. And whether it's there or not, I am a proud, card-carrying Scouser!

The commercial work was frowned upon by the snootier fashionistas. Oh, bite me! For the first time in my life I was having fun, making money and becoming independent from those who had been crushing the spirit out of me.

Meanwhile, back in London we went to endless parties including a weird and wonderful one called Kinky Gerlinky. I think it was Leigh Bowery's (a now deceased drag artist's) party, but I don't know for sure. I used to just smile and nod; I hadn't a clue about anything, but as a young girl I would rather have died than admit it. In hindsight my naivety was probably quite sweet, but I didn't allow myself to own up when I didn't know something. There were always wonderful, funny stylists and makeup artists who would grab you and dress you up. Dick Page, Jalle Bakka, Jimo Salako and Pat McGrath were my favourites. They would paint me and dress me outrageously. It was so much fun, I was like their little doll. I also met a model called Roy and a choreographer called Les Child, both of whom were doing the shows, and they looked after me. I had no idea where any of them were now until recently, again the monster web. We used to go to a club called The Wag long before footballer's wives and girlfriends were given the 'WAG' moniker.

Like all young girls, I was insecure, but even more so because of my battery of problems. I remember going for a night out with a large group. Among them was a model who will remain nameless, though he knows who he is. He was with an agency called Rage off the Harrow Road and was black with a shaved head. He was very polite and well-spoken and was one of the many familiar faces I would see at the shows and walk around the streets with on 'go sees'. He was another ambitious model, but was a bit older than the rest of us.

I think I went to The Wag club with him, or Kinky Gerlinky or Browns; somewhere in the West End. We were with a group, all drinking and having fun. When it was time for me to go home we hopped in a cab together. Not many people from that scene lived in South East London. West London certainly and South West London at a push, but the South East was too working class, too ragamuffin. I still have a home there to this day, because that's the area I identify with.

I was grateful because I was too drunk to get the night bus, which I usually would have done. In the cab I felt really, really strange, I couldn't even hold my head up. It was out of character for me to get bladdered like this. I knew how to look after myself and hadn't drunk that much because I had thought I would be getting the bus.
The next thing I remember is him climbing off me. I was coming round in my own flat and he was dismounting me; I don't know how else to put it. I had just been 'date raped'. I was numb, scared, humiliated, and too terrified about what had just happened to speak, never mind call rape. Bizarrely, being the perfect hostess, I think I even walked him to the door in a state of shock. I've never really got over that.

Then I scrubbed myself inside and out with a scourer, scalding myself with boiling hot water. I sat in the bathtub crying until I could think about what I should do next. He was someone I knew, so how could it be rape? I was drunk, so who would take me seriously? I sat in the bath for about sixteen hours, oblivious to how cold the water had become. The phone rang and it was the same vile male model asking me if he could see me again. I wondered if I was going mad! Did he think we went on a date? I'm almost sure he spiked my drink because when he was on top of me I was out cold! The phone rang again and this time it was my sister. The man I had had a crush on all my teenage years – the brother of the guys I lived with when I first got to London – had been shot dead in Liverpool: six times, in the back. Yes, on paper he was a drug dealer, and yes he was a bully. Yes he was a "bad" man and a womaniser. But I didn't see him like that. He was nicer to me than the people I lived with in Liverpool. He was lots of unexpected things: a poet and an artist; someone who loved karate; a hilariously funny guy; and the first to see any beauty in me. My sister broke the news with her usual sledgehammer sensitivity: "Guess what? ... is dead!" This harshness accompanies our background; the survivor is naturally numb in emotional terms.

I then recall receiving a phone call from my father. Ironically, the timing seemed perfect. Perhaps I imagined that since we shared the same birthday he was connected to me after all and that he was going to swoop in and make everything alright. I was told out of the blue that my father was going to call me and I remember sitting tensely by the phone. I was nineteen and wondered with real anticipation what was he going to say. The phone rang at the appointed time and I wrenched it from the cradle.

"Hello?" His voice was gravelly and he had a beautiful, deep Nigerian accent. After such a long wait I wasn't emotionally equipped for this vocal reunion, so I let him lead. "Where is the money from the house we lived in in Liverpool?" he asked. I was absolutely devastated, but I quipped: "Mum spent every penny of it bringing us up!" Not being able to see the irony in this, he carried on undaunted: "Make sure you don't fight with your brother." It was like he was talking to a three-year-old girl and was just calling to check on me after popping out for a moment, having just left me with a babysitter. There was no recognition of the fact he had gone and never looked back, that sixteen years had passed, and was only calling now to find drink or bail-out money. It was absolutely bizarre. Some people should not be allowed to have kids! I think it was this that tipped me over the edge.

I started to pack my stuff, randomly and madly. Even though I was desperately wounded at this point, it took a lot for me to break rank. My family was very close-knit and none of us had ever done anything like that. But I had had an invitation from Lorri who was living in California and it seemed like a brilliant idea to me. In the blink of an eye I was gone. I didn't plan to return to London.

I have never seen that male model again. More importantly, I never told anyone until 2006, when I told my then soon-to-be-husband with fear and trepidation in my heart. In a bid for intimacy, I didn't want to have any secrets from him. Come on, who would I tell? I probably would have got hysteria from my mother and never been allowed out of her sight again. She would have been horrified by my broken innocence.

I was striving for independence and safety big time and wanted to flee the memories, so if telling her had kept me bound in any way I would have considered it a fate worse than death. This new blow from my father tipped the scales and got me out of the disabling fear of the unknown. Who was available to comfort me or to help me work it all out? The Lord was, but even though he knew me, I hadn't remembered Him at this point.

Chapter Five: Run rabbit, run rabbit, run, run, run!

So I decided to go and live in America under the guise of seeing my friend. I was really going to seek my fortune, to become a fashion model, but I couldn't tell anybody that. I got it wrong as at first I went to Los Angeles, since the only person I knew in America lived there. This is laughable in fashion terms, since everyone knows the fashion capital of the US is New York. Well, everybody but me. I was an unsophisticated Scouser, honey, and didn't know much about anything. My naivety protected me and gave me the childlike courage to venture out. By mistake I joined a 'glamour agency', that's what the Americans called page three! I thought the boobs on the girls I saw were a little large! Silly me, I was a gel-needing 34B at the best of times. But hey, I was a kid and was desperate to escape my family, Liverpool and the limits that the British fashion industry had placed on me. I'm still trying.

As I said before, there was one black superstar at this time: Naomi Campbell. I love her because she gave me the confidence to go out and try. I love her body of work. OK, I love her body too – not in a Liberty Baker (my lesbian character from Footballers' Wives) kind of way, but just for the fact that God really did a good job when he assembled her! She is fabulous, and to this day she excels. She has created images of such breathtaking beauty and, despite all the negative press, I love her because she dared to try. For me she represents the pioneer spirit, the willingness to try. The first one over the fence, she took many slings and shots for those of us who came up behind her hoping, and for that I will be eternally grateful. Having said that, trying to break in was very frustrating because she was the chosen one; the industry had no room for another black, full-lipped girl. Daunted, but not one to be dictated to, I set about finding another way to pursue my dream of becoming someone.

It was a blessing in disguise that I had nowhere else to turn as things at home were going from bad to worse. My poor mother was rumoured to have had a nervous breakdown as a result of the brutality she had suffered under my father's alcoholic hand. Alcohol itself is a mindbender, so I'm not exaggerating when I say I come from a family plagued with mental illness, although this has never been medically certified.

My mother, God love her, hides her insanity with drama: mostly verbal misunderstandings, accusations, petty court cases, overeating, hilarity, problems with people and endless 419s. You know that email that gets sent around about a family inheritance in Nigeria that will give you the lion's share of two million pounds in exchange for your bank account details? If I didn't know how crap she was with computers I would swear that she had initiated it, because it's classic 419.

419 is petty and debilitating, especially when it is done in your name. I don't know why my mother always uses her kids' names, but I guess that's the real touch of insanity. If she was saner she'd at least make some fictional names up, but as it is she uses ours again and again. She has used each of our names on cars, utility bills, houses, businesses, at the doctors to get free prescriptions, and the list goes on. That's typically the way we were raised: to survive at any cost; to distract, cheat, cover up, fake it and lie! It didn't matter as long as you got what you wanted.

I once asked my brother why things were like that and he freaked me out. He reminded me what our childhood was really like. I couldn't remember any of these things until he said a few choice words and it all came flooding back. As a result of the consistent terror my mother experienced she was temporarily insane and developed crazy ways of coping. I realise now that we were really emotionally tortured as children and my brother reminded me how our mother claimed she was constantly followed by a fictitious character called Francis E. According to her, he was so in love with her that, because she had rejected him, he was willing to drug and hurt her. She claims he stalked her for thirty years and was the one responsible for breaking up her marriage by getting her husband drunk. So she had to be careful at all times and obviously so did we.

Another time I happened to be at her house. There was a dreaded letter from the courts about a missing TV licence and it was in my name. I already a licence in my name for my own address, but my name was now on the chopping block at her address. There were also cars in my name that needed verification and I called her on it. She went mad, attack being her first line of defence, and then relented saying she was 'handling' it, that it was a mistake. Then there was the usual pleading: "Don't touch it, don't do anything", blah, blah, blah.

Based on history and previous misappropriations of my name, it was clear my mother had provoked the stream of bailiffs that had come and gone. It doesn't take a genius to figure out her intentions, but it's so bloody tiring to keep fighting off the mess she lobs at your life. Now don't get me wrong, she loves us and we love her, I know I do; that's where my damage stems from. It's hard to understand the complexity of someone who, on the one hand would do anything for you, but on the other does so many things that leave you almost mortally wounded. For one reason or another she cannot control herself.

My mum had invested in a nail salon in South London. She had come to Los Angeles to see me and we would always get our nails done, so she was ahead of the game. But this was the early nineties before people got acrylic nails on mass, so she preempted the trend by about a decade. That would have been fine if it hadn't been for the fact she can't do nails! Surprise, surprise, it went bust, but I love that she has never allowed her misfortune to stop her from trying stuff. She is one courageous lady.

Later still, when I arrived home from the States one time, I found out that someone had used my name, or a very similar one, for the shop my mum had run, which had been declared bankrupt. What a coincidence! Fortunately, I was able to prove that I had been living in America and my name was cleared.

No surprises then that I have found myself going through life initially being unable to be close to anyone, because if this is how your beginnings are, you will naturally have difficulty trusting people. But thankfully those early lessons haven't prevented me from having wonderful friendships and people in my life. It's been a slow process but I maintain that it can be done. I still have panic attacks and I think I chose the modelling career and ultimately became an actress to create a different reality; to overcome my fears and perhaps to become untouchable, impervious to pain. I guess I wanted to be anyone apart from the scared girl growing up in that mad house.

My brother reminded me that my mother had all these strange issues with colours and would feel very threatened if someone was connected with the colour red. He reminded me that she was extremely verbally aggressive with us, and whenever someone called for us as children she would scream loudly in Ibo, slam doors in their faces and generally terrorise them. It was humiliating to even try to have friends call at the house for you. She is actually pretty harmless, but when stressed she's about as 'funny' as Jack Nicholson in The Shining. My brother reminded me that she was a storyteller and always liked to be at the centre of intrigue. He explained that this is the same kind of torture prisoners are subjected to; where the paradigm is psychologically shifted all the time, and this suggested to me that we were possibly all suffering from post-traumatic stress.

We have all found different ways of dealing with the madness. Mind you, it has been hidden and coped with in a myriad of ways. My brother was reportedly addicted to street heroin (or brown as it is called), although I heard from someone else it was crack. Who knows, I've never seen him take it. Drug wise I couldn't tell whether it was true or not because it's all foreign to me. I was busy trying to deal with my own wounds in the US, but the rumours abound. Sadly, he has spent most of his life on the wrong side of the law: raging and going in and out of the penal system. But I have also noticed the way the penal system has exploited him. He may have done things to get into trouble, but in recent years I have also watched him be brutalised by the police. For a while now he has been doing well, but the 'justice' system has his name and number and constantly calls him back inside. He has been unjustly sentenced and held against his will many times for doing absolutely nothing. I have very mixed emotions about him because I still see him as a beautiful and lovely person in many ways. He's a great laugh and a real character; someone I love very deeply. He can be hard work and these imprisonments have obviously taken their toll on him and on the family unit. I have fretted and worried about him to the point that I was unable to function after coming back from the States. At this point he was all I thought about, even with all the great work stuff that was unfolding in my own life.

I couldn't understand why I wasn't able to save him. Each incarceration caused another fight about what should be done to help, about who isn't doing enough. Then one sister would always complain that she didn't get the same kind of help, which is mind-blowing. Obviously you give more help to those that need it, right? Whatever the cause, the results have made his survival very difficult and then some loophole in the system comes and drags him back under. I noticed that during my time away he went from being a man who was very uncommunicative, quiet and perhaps a bit dodgy but mostly harmless, to a man who was completely isolated from the rest of the world. He's on the edge and very lost, but still loyal. I actually think he is ill, 'soul tired', maybe from dealing with our mother. It's hard to get a job when you have as many holes in your CV as my brother, having spent most of his life in and out of correctional facilities. Do you lie? Do you make up experiences? Or do you tell the truth and have the person who was about to give you a job just roll their eyes and move on? Similarly, it's hard to get a regular job when you've spent your life pursuing the arts. No one believes you really want the menial job they're offering when they've seen your name in the credits on TV, despite the fact you are tired of waiting for the next big break. So I can relate to his struggle a lot.

My two sisters and I exhibited what psychiatrists call classic 'triangle behaviour'. Whoever is not there gets absolutely pasted, slagged off and verbally beaten, then the remaining two feel relieved at first, then 'spent', and then finally perhaps a little better about their own lot. One of my sisters talks quite endlessly about family dysfunction: how unhappy her childhood was, how hard done by she was, how little she was thought of; and chronicling (in minute detail) everyone's faults and foibles. This turns into a tongue-lashing about the other sister and then we feel bad when we hang up the phone. So sometimes I make her angry with me so she won't talk to me for a while, just to give me a rest from the cycle. But mostly I feel that I am the outsider, set apart as my mother's favourite.

I didn't think there was anything wrong with us when I was little; I was loved and blissfully ignorant. It's only since I've grown up and travelled that I can see things as they were. Even knowing what I know now, I am cheered slightly by the knowledge that all families are dysfunctional. Everyone has skeletons in the closet. I am entirely sure, given the way I've behaved over the years, that I'm not exempt from Oruche madness, to be fair. My way of dealing with the brokenness was to lap up media attention, be it modelling pictures or acting jobs. I was trying to fill the void, to heal the fractures, the messes and the legacy of subtle but ever-present abuse by having the world salute me. I was trying to get the love I should have had at home from the workplace, which generally means you are on a hiding to nothing. I was still pathetically trying to gain approval from my mad family, angry all the while that I wasn't living up to my full potential. I am still the same girl. I still want to be protected from the responsibility of provision. This "gimme gimme… I need help" approach comes from my mum.

I don't fully know what has happened to her in life because she is a pathological storyteller, but I do know she was an abused woman, a woman battered by her alcoholic husband, so I have compassion. Genetically I can only choose between her nurture and my dad's alcoholic nature, so given all that I haven't done too badly!

I love my mother because she is still inherently good. A weaker woman would have abandoned us to children's homes or institutions, but she stood by us in a foreign land where she was the underdog and unable to get work. I don't condone her ways of 'making it', but I certainly understand why she felt the need for the scams, despite the fact that they produced a legacy of hurt, battered and bruised children.

Initially I thought my dream was purely about getting away from my family, the poverty and the teen pregnancies that I saw around me. This was the lot in life for the average black teenager in Liverpool. But armed with Naomi's guts and Bill Cosby's vision for the dream family I didn't have, I finally realised what I wanted.

I went to the States because I badly wanted to succeed and escape all of that. I hoped that each trophy and talisman I collected for my artistic or modelling endeavours would fix me somehow. Not a chance. There was a God-shaped hole in me and only God could fill it.

When you are young you have no notion of departing from the family norm. You may know that something is different about your family, even wrong perhaps, and mine was definitely different from other families. But honestly, in my Scouse, childlike frankness and naivety I thought my mother's behaviour was just an immigrant thing, the result of culture shock. Like all good con women, she is so compelling, so charming, so funny, sweet and kind. She is generous to a fault, always helping people out, whether she has the means to or not.

I've always been my mother's favourite. Actually, it would be more accurate to say that my brother and I were favoured over my sisters, poor girls! But as we grew, and after I had left for America, she and my brother ground each other down with abuse and badly hatched schemes. He fell out of her good favour, which he couldn't see for the blessing that this was. Instead she turned her myopic eyes towards me and my success as a talisman for her eroded self-esteem. She started to build a pedestal that, frankly, is hard to balance on. She gets off on my success and always annihilates me when I don't do well, despite the fact she has contributed to my downfall on many occasions.

I went to America hoping the streets would be paved with gold. I had sold my white Ford XR2, my first modelling trophy, and stayed with Lorri in Venice beach. She told me she was living in a hotel, but she had exaggerated, bless her. She had missed out the 's' and was actually living in a hoStel! As in, you pay for a bed and have no control over who shares your room. Even though I was raised on a council estate, I had started modelling, travelling and enjoying reasonable success, so I was filled with the inflated ego that the first rush of success brings. I had left my one-room council flat behind in South East London and let go of a rent-paying tenant so my sister could have a studio to 'create' in. (Ah, the stupidity of youth! I gamely left it in the hands of my mum and sister, and they ran up all kinds of bills in my name so I couldn't return. I got what I deserved, I should have left the lovely tenant alone, but family dictates that you must help at all costs and that their lack of planning is ALWAYS your emergency.)

I had only known subsidised housing and school dinners, but I had delusions of grandeur and was not impressed with Lorri's accommodation. I was very impressed with Venice Beach though: the sun, the sand, the sea. It all felt very sexy to me, but the prize of life was the boardwalk and, initially, the American way of life. Everybody seemed so free.

Outrageously dressed people were everywhere, and there were people of all ages skating down the boardwalk, from scantily dressed nubile blonde chicks and surfer dudes to much older, unfortunately still scantily clad, women and men! There was no British reserve here and I realised very quickly that if there was anywhere I could get out of my box, reinvent and become all that I wanted to be, it was in America. So that's what I set out to do.

Anyway, back to the glamour agency that had signed me on and wanted me to get a boob job. I was cheered on by the prospect of a pay check and modelling work so I signed up with the agency but told them to leave my boobs alone, thank you very much! I didn't realise at this point that they had to sponsor for the sake of your immigration papers, and that they then owned you in a sense because you couldn't work for anyone else.

So Lorri had given me my first place to stay in LA, even if it was a hostel. And my new friend Kim, who was thirtyish at the time, was older and much wiser than me. I thought at the time that she was ancient and the oracle! She gave me the much-needed counsel and support I needed to get started in LA when I arrived with my tiny collection of belongings. I hadn't thought it through at all. I had no apartment planned, for example, so we set up our new lives together. I got a flat next door to her and basically copied what she did until I found my own way. She was my guide. I had youth and enthusiasm, but she was invaluable in teaching me the ropes.

Chapter Six: Say it loud! I am black, and I am proud!

I finally realised that if I wanted to do fashion I had to go to the fashion capital, where all the magazines were based. At the same time, as fate would have it, I was spotted in Glen Jones' "Here we go again" music video, in which I played his love interest in LA. This prompted the interest of Essence magazine, and its staff started hunting me down! Through a string of God-inspired 'coincidences' and the kindness of strangers, they eventually found me.

They sent me a ticket to Twentynine Palms, which was also in California, to do a magazine cover test shoot. I was up against another model, Lorraine Pascal, who I was quite intimidated by. She had London in the palm of her hand when we left and was with prestigious model agency Models One, whose owners had earlier laughed at my constant attempts to try and become a model. So for the cover to be between me and her was terrifying. I was sure she would get it, but I was happy to be asked. We went to do the shoot and to my surprise I got the cover. They decided I was to be on the September 1992 cover, which is quite an honour because September is the most important fashion edition. I remember the fashion editor saying that if I wanted to come to New York to do some fashion pages then I should look them up. That was all I needed to get pumped up. Wow!

I contacted Essence and, true to form, they organised a shoot for me, so off I went to NYC. The airline had lost my bags so I turned up to the shoot looking like a tomboy with short dreadlocks and leggings that I had worn for so long they were shiny and baggy at the knees! Roxanna Floyd, a makeup artist, took me to dinner and then all over New York. I literally became part of her family and I am proud to say I've been her little sister ever since.

God knew I needed support and he brought it to me in the form of this wonderful, godly woman. Roxanna had had a secure upbringing – church was a big part of her world – but I didn't necessarily attribute that to how well she had made it through life. In one year she did eleven of the twelve Essence magazine covers. Essence was like a black beauty bible and was the first platform to endorse me, giving me a cover and featuring me prominently in their fashion pages over the years. I thank them for my rapid rise on the New York scene. Ironically, the only Essence cover Roxanna didn't do the makeup for that year was mine, but she befriended me anyway. She worked on Queen Latifah, Angela Bassett and Whitney Houston's makeup, doing eleven major motion pictures—always at the star's request. It was quite unusual for a magazine makeup artist to cross over into film, but the fact that she did so was testimony to her greatness. And the fact the stars themselves requested her, and did battle to get her, spoke volumes. She owned a lovely condo in New York and yet she was totally normal. She didn't have any of the phoney airs and graces the fashion and entertainment industries are famous for.

I was blessed with a penthouse on Fifth Avenue. It was owned by a photographer, who said that if I pretended to be his cousin from Jamaica I could rent it from him for a tiny amount of rent. I had met him through his wife, who was the fashion editor on the cover shoot, and I really feel now that it was God's protection for me. My agent Bethann, who became my adoptive new mother, paid the rent, which she would later take from my earnings as a model. It was a tall building with a doorman and elevators! When I explained how and where I was living to other young models they were surprised because the rent was so miniscule. I used to take taxis everywhere and get my nails done at $70 a pop. This was seventeen years ago, so they must have seen me coming!

We used to joke that we all had an empty fridge, and the only required items were a bottle of vodka and a tin of cat food for the many cats roaming New York we adopted. I felt like I had landed in heaven and I was right: God was setting in motion the greatest victory a poor and abused young girl could ever have entered into. This was my finishing school, but there were a lot of rough edges to take off. Nevertheless, there I was at twenty-two living in New York City!
And I was a much sought-after fashion model. I was very proud of the fact that I had come from nothing and was being used to emphasise

beauty, fashion and mainstream products. But as proud as I was, something wasn't quite right. Oh, I could play along with the best of them; I was stylish now! I had a wonderful designer wardrobe, did all the shows in Bryant Park and walked the runway with the best of them.

The only person I never worked with, to my regret, was Cindy Crawford. I would have liked to learn from her as she's a great model. In a way I was glad that I didn't get to meet her, though. I was too much of a fan and would have gone all sycophantic and frothed at the mouth. I did that once with Prince and it was not a pretty sight! I was spared that with Cindy.

I remember how we looked down on certain New York postcodes. How did I have had the nerve, you ask? I know! This was the bravado of youth and a very short memory. You had to live on the West Side, not the East Side; in Manhattan and not any of the other boroughs. There were specific books that everyone had on their coffee tables. I can't remember what they were now, but no one had read them, you just had to have them. It was a mad, pretentious little society. Like all the other 'circus runaways', I wanted to fit in with these mad rules and I did my best. But I have to say that, as always, I knew my own mind, so I would play along in theory while rolling my eyes mentally.

People that I worked with for a day became my 'friends', but underneath all the pretence I was quite shy and hated the fact that everyone was so fly-by-night; that they couldn't be relied upon and were always scrabbling onto the next thing. In LA they call this BBD: bigger, better deal. People weren't committed to you and I was the same, completely noncommittal. Did I enjoy it a lot of the time? Yes. The money was incredible and I wish I had that kind of money coming in now that I'm more mature.

There were always fashion shows, club openings, book signings and events happening that you had to go to. I hated them and would obsess terribly over each appearance. But I wanted to do the right thing and these events always seemed to be of paramount importance, so I also hated not going for fear I would be passed over for work. If someone mentioned that something had been 'fabulous' and I hadn't been there I felt physically sick. I needed the approval of these people. Around this time, the travelling, the emptiness and the missing out on my family's lives started to take its toll. I once even sent an airline ticket to my three-year-old nephew because I really loved and missed him and wanted him to come out. Ultimately, as a result of one misunderstanding or another, he wasn't allowed to come.

I even tried to look up my father. I was born on his birthday, and I wanted to know him. I was curious about him and figured that since I didn't mesh well with my siblings, maybe my father could help me unravel the differences. This was good in theory.

I flew my mother to Nigeria from London and I met her there from NYC. I made sure her flight landed first because I needed her to be there when I landed and with me every step of the way. I enlisted my mother's help because she spoke Ibo and I didn't, and of course I really needed a familiar reference point in case things went crazy, which of course they did. My mother was frightened of seeking him out, and she later told me that although she might not have had much over the years, she had at least had freedom from him.

We were staying at my cousin Pee's house. She was a powerful minister of the gospel in her own right, so our time was not our own. Add the intermittent phone signal, the militia rule and the power cuts that the government doled out to the population and we could see that this was not going to work, even though Pee was fortunate enough to have her own generator for when the power cuts struck.

Truthfully speaking, the mayhem caused at night when the government turned off the power was incredible. The first thing I remember was one of the night security guards coming in crying one morning because his sister had died in hospital the night before. The generators went off and the machine that was maintaining her breathing went off too. It was madness that we could have a generator to keep our lights on at home, but people in the hospital were dying.

These were the circumstances under which I embarked on the quest for my father. I wasn't successful, although I did manage to find out that he was in hospital with a liver condition. I was given the phone number, but whenever I tried to call I wasn't able to get through. I'm grateful for this now as I probably would have had my heart smashed to smithereens, but at the time I was devastated.

I know now that people who abuse substances are unable to choose you first; it's not because of you, but because of the thorns in their flesh. I wanted a fairytale ending, but I'm convinced now that I wouldn't have got one had we met. I would have got hit up for money and rejected, so I feel the Lord protected me from that one. I had had enough madness and rejection from my family and it was being added to daily by the fashion industry. If I had not been prevented from meeting up with him, I would have shattered emotionally. Eight months later he was dead; I was told the news over the phone by my older sister – the bearer of bad news – and one of my long-lost cousins on my father's side. What I found hard was that they could find me to tell me he was dead, but not to tell me how ill he was. That hurt more than the usual disorganised dysfunction. If I had known he was ailing perhaps I could have done something.

Even then I mourned in a way that I found embarrassing. I realise now it was the loss of a sense of promise I was mourning. I had always thought I would find my father and that when I did all would be right in my world. Fortunately, I was consoled by work as New York loved me at that time; the African American market loved the fact that I was African and had natural, short, dreadlocked hair, which was the hair of the moment. Being embraced by the African American market and population did wonders for my self-esteem, which is wonderful when you're 'up'. But self-esteem built on human praise is a hiding to nothing and when the tide turns, and it always does, the crash to the ground is as all-encompassing as the high. I have endured equal measures of both and have subsequently learned to put my trust in the esteem that only God can give me.

After I made it onto the cover of Essence, people suddenly started asking me for my autograph, my opinions, and asking me to parties; largely believing that I was a militant black because I didn't wear hair extensions! This wasn't true; I am not a politically minded person at all. It was very strange because on the inside I was still the battered chick from the hood, and just because I had ended up in a public job, it didn't mean I had the brains or experience to advise or help anyone. Around that time I started getting fan mail – tons and tons of it. People started recognising me in the street and, while embarrassing, I could just about deal with it. But I also had prisoners writing me letters. I remember one in particular where the prisoner asked me if I could call Bill Cosby, Oprah and several of my other high-profile celebrity friends and get them to secure his release. In his limited understanding, me being on the cover of a magazine meant I must be very well connected, like a senator of something. I remember musing over it, feeling for him and even identifying with his need. But I realised that if I did ever get any of these people on my speed dial, at that time of my life I would have been focused on my next job, not his parole. It was quite a mixed bag: I loved the validation, but felt uncomfortable with the assumption that I could be all things to all people.

I was fortunate to get a Gap account shot by fashion photographer Patrick Demarchlier. I recently had an interesting time reminiscing when I saw he had done all the photo shoots with Sarah Jessica Parker for the Sex in the City movie. To all intents and purposes, Carrie personifies my experience of New York. It was very strange working with him at the time, as the coup of getting to work with him was massive, as was the pressure. I didn't know then that there is no such thing as superstars, that people are people, no matter what their publicists have done to hype them, or where their status rests in life. We come in naked and go out the same way, no matter what we amass. If I had known that I might have enjoyed myself more. I don't think he even spoke to me as his native French was impossible to understand. But he still shot the best picture ever taken of me up to that point because I think he really understood the shyness and inexperience that most people didn't see; he saw behind the façade I was using to protect myself from pain.

I loved this part of my life because I made my mother proud. She loved being in NYC and seeing me all over everything. It was quite a moment for both of us. She told me that when she saw me on the back of a bus in London on a GAP advert, she missed me so much that she followed the bus a long way just to look at me and actually ended up getting lost! Awwww!

I also got to work with my 'idols': Waris Dirie in Puerto Rico, and Stephanie Roberts in Milan for Complice, a Dolce and Gabbana line. I was paired with Waris a lot as she was East African and I was West African. We were short-haired, mock tough girls and we had a laugh together. She was very changeable emotionally, though, in fact she made my journey through life seem like a walk in the park. I haven't seen her for years, but I really respect her.

One season the fashion industry decided to use only black models, which was why there were so many of us. It was a lovely time because we normally didn't get to work together; we were normally pitted against one another. That was the first and only time I had the guts to go to Milan for Italy's fashion week. Tyra Banks asked me once: "Phina, how come you don't go to Italy? How come you don't do the shows?" The truth was I was afraid and lacked confidence. I thought I had pushed my luck as far as it would go. If I thought of God at all, I thought of Him as many of us do in terms of human kindness, believing there is only so much He will dutifully dole out to you for your good behaviour, minus your sins. So I quipped: "Oh, I'll do Italy…" as matter-of-factly as I could. I didn't realise just how prophetic those words would prove to be.

I shot the cover of the Washington Post with George Holz in Cancun. It was the trip of a lifetime; us models rode horses on the beach in bikinis in our spare time.

Chapter Seven: All that glitters is not gold

I guess I have the heart of a gambler, because anyone else would have been happy to come from nothing and crack NYC, but not me. I have memories of such glamour and magnitude there; models were invited everywhere. I remember going to the première of Malcolm X and the subsequent party in the Roseland Ballroom, I mean, come on: it was the quintessential list of who's who. Spike Lee, Diana Ross and Stevie Wonder were there, and of course Denzel Washington and Wesley Snipes; all the New York stars and DJs of the time attended. The LA Super Rap set had flown in and I danced with Snoop Dogg. Whenever he saw me, Dr Dre always said: "Hey, ain't you that model?" I got to know Queen Latifah before she ever made a film and there was an English rapper I knew called Monie Love. Heavy D was there, as was Super Cat from Jamaica, who I had done a music video with, and Q-Tip from A Tribe called Quest. I spent time with De la Soul and Living Color and was on great terms with Karen Wheeler of Soul II Soul.

Bethann had really taken me under her wing: she handed me the keys to all things black and beautiful in NYC. A former model herself, she also had dreadlocks, so she took placing me in the best, non-traditional adverts a black woman could get involved in very seriously. Bethann had three houses: one in NYC, one in upstate New York and another in Antigua. Seeing her and Roxanna's lifestyles, my concept of what a black woman could achieve was blown sky high. Forget handouts, the dole, housing benefit and tax credits! Now don't get me wrong, there is no shame in collecting benefits if that's where you are now, I've been there myself. But Bethann taught me that you don't have to remain at a level you don't want to, especially when your status is based on other people's perceptions of you.

I also benefited from the experience of my agent Bethann being the mother (and manager) of Kadeem Hardison from A Different World, which was my favourite show as a teenager. I chose my agent based on a TV show; that shows you how young I was. But what can I tell you? It worked, and it worked well! I appealed to a niche market and

she had a stable of great black models including Gary Dourdan, who later went on to star in CSI and Tyson Beckford, who broke new ground when he was contracted by Ralph Lauren; this was very normal for a white man but unprecedented for a black one.
It was a prosperous time. I was making about $100,000 a year doing commercials, adverts and catalogues. I made many trips to the Caribbean and the rest of the world doing music videos before they just became booty shakers for black women.

So when I started to grow dissatisfied, Roxanna and Bethann both told me I was making a stupid mistake, and hindsight has helped me to see their point. But I did what I had to do at the time. The sadness, the rape, the abuse and the brokenness were never quite held at bay by all this extremely fabulous but shallow external stuff. What I needed was God; I just didn't know it.

Bethann even came round to my apartment, the one she had paid for in lieu of my earnings several years before. She had given me a start in life and here I was being totally ungrateful, leaving her agency largely because a load of other girls from London had started to show up and what I was doing didn't seem special to me anymore. Perhaps the mere presence of these girls triggered memories of what I was running from. There were two in particular – in hindsight I'm sure they were both lovely women – who inadvertently seemed to create the hideous triangle that existed between me and my sisters.

I don't know what is was, but I found myself going down to the agency and "borrowing my portfolio to show a client" then legging it home in a taxi and calling them to say I had left. There was no other way they would ever have released my book, because whenever you left an agent they badmouthed you and hid your book, claiming it was lost because they couldn't bring themselves to wish you well. You were worth too much as a model and people got really nasty when you changed direction.

Bethann was on my doorstep in a New York minute. I mean, at this point I was a high earner. You know you're doing well when you have a personal banker so you don't have to wait in line. It was "Miss Oruche this, Miss Oruche that!" They see you coming and roll out the red carpet. That was the life she introduced me to.

So when I quit her agency she mock beat me up with a rolled up magazine, she was so convinced I was messing up my future. I kept thinking about the fact that I was alone at least eighty percent of the time, that the fashion industry was fickle, that every day I had to constantly look for work. Modelling jobs generally only last a day, a week tops, and the pressure to have beautiful clear skin, stay thin and get connected to the powerful was taking its toll. You always had to know who to schmooze and who not give the time of day to.

Plus, I didn't have a sophisticated bone in my body, so I couldn't enjoy New York the way I would probably enjoy it now. I didn't think I was worthy to go into posh restaurants and I thought most things were out of my league; that I was just a fearful little girl playing the part of a model. Because of this I spent an amazing amount of time on the phone trying to reconnect with fly-by-night models and friends I had met along the way.

I was getting further and further away from my family and although this was what I had wanted, it unhinged me somehow. They didn't understand when I complained about having to go to yet another country, yet another hotel. Most people's unlived fantasy is to be a jetsetter, but it takes its toll. Why do you think so many people in the entertainment industry start to crack up or end up with substance abuse problems? It's hard to keep changing time zones, to miss everyone's birthdays, to miss out on nieces and nephews growing up and lives happening, and to have everybody miss yours. It's horrible not being able to sleep because you are still jetlagged from Paris and are leaving for Los Angeles the next day. It's hard when you get home to New York to a message that sends you right back out to Paris to do the collections only to get cancelled when you arrive because you're too short, flat-chested, spotty or ugly. I was fortunate that not much of that happened to me.

I got to do the Chanel show with Naomi, Linda, Cindy, Claudia, Christy, Carla Bruni(now Mrs sarkozy!), and Kate Moss. I was also lucky enough to do the Christian Lacroix show while black comedy Prêt a Porter was being filmed. Sophia Loren made all of us look like teenage boys with her buxom fabulousness. She even dwarfed the sexuality and grace of her co-stars, Kim Bassinger and the legendary Lauren Bacall.

But while all this was going on, I also saw teenagers being destroyed around me. I watched the predators come and take the girls. The older, wealthy men, including some famous movie stars, would make alliances with the modelling agencies and, in a sense, girls as young as fourteen would become high-class hookers. Mummy and daddy were in a small town, a safe distance away, thinking their little girl was doing really well in the big city because she talked a good game and sent nice pictures home. But I often watched the girls who had no financial sense get robbed in lots of different ways. They racked up bike bills for the books that had to go quickly from one buyer to the next. They were all charged the full cost of the bike rather than it being split between the number of books on the bike. They were also charged for fictional promos and all the Lincoln Town Cars that took us to and from airports and appointments. Costs would pile up and if you weren't smart you would lose count of the number you owed for.

I learned how the girls were pumped with drugs so that they developed habits and didn't care how much money they received so long as their habits were fed. There were many late-night dinners with clients and important men. You never really knew what these men did, or why it was so important to schmooze them.

One night I watched in horror as a young girl of maybe thirteen was carried out of a party by several fat, old, bald men. I can only imagine what happened to her, since I know what had happened to me several years before. I drank myself but made it my business to keep it in check because I had already seen the devastation alcohol caused when it went unchecked. I have lived my life with a genuine fear of alcohol and still haven't really made my peace with it.

I wanted to do something that would express who I was more fully than this. Plus I didn't particularly want to reach the top in a nasty business that would put me out to pasture at twenty-five! I lived opposite the Lee Strasberg Theatre and Film Institute in New York and really wanted to be an actor but, having already exceeded my wildest imaginings, I feared I had probably pushed my luck as far as possible. But that school taunted me every day. I don't know how long it took, but I eventually went in between bookings and enrolled!

So it was time for me to go back to school and learn the craft of acting rather than just talking about it. I was terrified; I mean really terrified.

Chapter Eight: Cast me if you can

I didn't understand acting; I didn't get the way you had to make yourself vulnerable. Where I came from vulnerability wasn't an option, you'd be eaten alive. I didn't understand the method acting taught by Lee Strasberg either. I had tried it when I was at the Institute because I lived across the street, but I was always being whisked away for modelling bookings and used that as an excuse not to practise my scenes and not to take it seriously. If I was too busy to practice my scenes, it couldn't be my fault if I was rubbish. That was a lose-lose situation, but I had an overblown idea of myself. I was on the wall in a Gap advert outside the theatre where we took our lessons, so I felt really important and wasted precious time. I was trying to be bigger than I felt, trying to be the girl in the photo rather than the nice, confused, lost little girl I truly was.

So to make the transition from model to actress I moved back to LA, thinking that if I broke into the film and television industry I would be all right, that I would be able to banish my insecurities forever. Let me pause to belly laugh at that ridiculous notion right here. Ha, ha, ha!

But there I was in Hollywood, Los Angeles; home of the movies. I had realised along the way that I wasn't happy just being a mute model. If you've ever met me you'll know that's true, people can barely get a word in edgewise!

When I called the Beverly Hills Playhouse (BHP) in LA they told me to come for an interview. They gave me a time and I said: "Well, OK, if I'm available that day and not on a modelling assignment, I'll show up." What a liberty! The woman on the phone very politely told me that this was a serious, very competitive business and that they didn't deal with people who had attitudes like mine. If only she had known I was faking it. All the "big girls" had these oversized attitudes so I thought it was the best way to show I had 'arrived'. As ever, it blew up in my face. That showed me! I was very interested in the class after that. Up until then I had done whatever I wanted, and the way my life was headed, it showed. I was hoping that acting would fill that ongoing hole in my soul. Yeah right!

By the time I got to BHP I was more humble and just wanted to work. Hollywood quickly showed me I was a nobody. So big deal, I had been in a few magazines. The black community recognised me, as we are supportive of our own and appreciate the struggle it takes to make it. But I quickly cottoned onto the fact that unless I perfected my craft I was going nowhere fast. I was taken into the best class because I had blagged to them that I could act. I didn't have a beginner's mentality back then.

In class I was fortunate enough to be taught by Jeffrey Tambor. He is the most amazing actor, his range is extraordinary. At the time he was filming The Larry Sanders Show, a big US hit. One day he said to me: "You are very talented." His pronouncement was like manna from heaven. How did he know? Was he sure? I wanted to ask him: "Are you talkin' to me?" Thinking about it logically now, I was surrounded by characters at home in England. I didn't even have to open the front door to encounter them. I was always in a swirl of drama at home, although admittedly a lot of it was self-created. People like me didn't usually act; it was a rare luxury for people from my background. But if you think about it, people like me should act given all the raw material and characters we're surrounded by. I thought that 'they' (who are 'they'?) would never let me do it and would laugh at me if I tried. Maybe 'they' were a special group of people who grew up in Chelsea. No, I'm serious, I really did think that. I didn't believe anyone would be allowed to excel if they had as many family problems and embarrassments as I did; if you were a 'no-mark' from Liverpool. Who are 'they' really though? That's the six million dollar question. 'They' are the people who you think will laugh at you if you fail; the people you think are watching your every move, just waiting to point the finger.

Anonymously toiling in my LA acting class I was broke. My salary had shrunk to twenty percent of what I had lived on for the previous three years. But I was happy initially. Modelling is me, me me, and you can't have that mentality if you want to survive as an actor. You need to listen, because you get most of what you are portraying from your acting partner. Listening was hard for me because I was so full of myself in the negative, insecure, 'do I look alright?' self-obsessed kind of way.

Gloria Gifford, another of my acting teachers from the BHP, told me: "Eat like a pig. They'll say you did anyway." Noted, I intended to. 'They' actually don't exist, they're a figment of your imagination, but it takes venturing out and taking chances to know that. Even if they do exist, they're certainly not thinking about you!

I was careful never to speak to my older sister about my dreams or fears. If I told her I was homesick or financially afraid for the future, she always said things like: "Well come home then, no one told you to go and live over there". One time, after I had been in America for years and she came to visit, she told me: "You're a broke superstar". Even after successful breakthroughs on hit shows like Buffy the Vampire Slayer, she made it clear my continued success wasn't ensured. Man that hurt, truthful though it was. But I couldn't quit. Support is everything to an artist, but she wasn't able to give me a simple "you can do it". Over the years she has changed a great deal in that regard. Perhaps she was just fearful for her little sister. She now calls me Miss D, the 'D' being for 'determined', as she always says that I can get anything done now. Recently, she was the first to coax me back into the (acting) game when I was gun-shy. Though the going got tough, I just got tougher and more resourceful. I was spurred on by the fact that I honestly had nothing and nowhere to go back to.

My mother's temporary insanity, my brother's brutality, the unwed baby mothers back home and the Naomi 'roadblock' loomed large. I wanted more out of my life, so I jumped from the frying pan into the fire. Occasionally I tried to run back to modelling in NYC, but it got to the point where I was too far removed from it. My pictures were too old, I was too old. I was too short, too African-looking; there was that whole mess again. I couldn't be bothered to fight the same battles all over again. I should have left the modelling door open, but at that point in my life I was a bridge-burner. I had no business sense or manners. Come on, where would I have got these attributes from? I always spoke too candidly and I still do. I'm a little too frank and Scouse for most Americans.

Over the years I have almost managed to learn when to fight and when to shut up! I knew it would have taken the same old fight to break into modelling again – as it would to get an acting job – but I was no longer truly interested in modelling. Saying you were a model/actress was mirth-inducing, so I usually had to tone down the modelling bit anyway.

The studios in Hollywood were lined with the bones of models that had bitten the dust trying to act. I reckon this is because Hollywood mostly works on looks and they often trawled the model agencies looking for beauties but then put them in situations they had neither the training nor the character for. Since there were no studio "finishing school" systems in place, as there had been years before, most of the girls failed and I didn't want that. But I did actually get my first role that way. I got a small part from Sydney Pollack (may God rest his soul) in the remake of Sabrina, starring Harrison Ford and Julia Ormond.

Question: how do you get from a small town and a tough background, from being taunted and teased, to starring on TV? It's not a small step, I can tell you. First of all I had to get some self-esteem if I wanted a chance to win. My Bible tells me I must be a good steward of the little I have before God will make me ruler over much. So I had one choice: push forward with the acting. So push I did.

Milton Katselas, one of my most influential and ruthless acting teachers, often said: "A family is a tyranny ruled over by its sickest member." He should know, he created quite a sick one at the Beverly Hills Playhouse. But boy did I relate to that. My family felt pretty unhealthy to me as I got further and further away from them and the denial started to burst. Now why the heck am I banging on about my unfortunate beginnings in life? To make you feel sorry for me? Please! That's not my style. If given nothing but lemons in life, go make some tasty lemonade.

I'm saying it to illustrate that it doesn't matter where you come from in life; it's your destination that counts. I mention the fatherlessness, my brother tormenting me, the male model taking advantage of me and the trials and triumphs of the modelling game because they shaped my view of everything male-dominated and brought my self-esteem to a resounding low. I have spent my whole life alternately trying to impress and compete with men.

In America I found myself chasing dreams, hoping they would fulfil me. Would another magazine cover do it? Or a film? Or a TV series? The answer was always a resounding NO! Life has much more value than that, but I didn't know that initially. I had to find out the long, hard way. Thank God for youth and ambition. The youth prevented me from thinking of the consequences and the ambition burned bright and acted like fuel; it kept me on track when the going invariably got tough.

Chapter Nine: Born to be wild

Whatever the situation, I am hard to correct. I used to take things really personally and get wounded very easily, which was absolutely the wrong spirit for this acting lark. I didn't understand or trust criticism, and didn't have the discernment to understand the difference between criticism and critique; I couldn't appreciate the difference between humility and humiliation.

Fortunately, I am healing beyond that, although to this day I have a problem with people telling me what to do. I have to control this because acting requires all kinds of people telling you what to do and I'm trying to learn how to humbly accept what they have to offer. The street taught me to have a chip on my shoulder, keep my chin raised and not let anybody affect me. You know the way teenagers are now: they don't get excited about anything. How sad! I was just like that.

I sat through twenty-hours of acting classes a week, which cost a fortune, and twenty-hours of rehearsal in my own free time. I stayed the course for five years in an extremely uncomfortable setting for my psyche, which demonstrates how driven I was to succeed. The first day and for several months afterwards, I went to class with all my demons. The inner turmoil of not being good enough to be there would manifest in a struggle.

The class was on Robertson Boulevard in LA and right next to it, on the corner of Gregory Way, was a Blockbuster video store. I used to spend so much time walking back and forth thinking, "I can't go in", turning on my heels and heading back to the car. But then I would say to myself, "I must go in" and turn back towards the class. The entire Blockbuster staff used to watch me with great amusement.

You can't emote if you have to keep up the stance of a bad girl with an emotionally vacant, rebellious stare. I thought I was a hard knock. I was running around Hollywood at that point with a micro-miniskirt, Guess knee-high boots, flowing dreadlocks and two pit bulls. When I wasn't driving my sky-blue Mercedes 450 SLC, that is. What was I thinking? All my worlds were colliding: the fashion world; the Hollywood freedom I found through the acting class; and my Toxteth beginnings. I must have looked a right state!

Thank God for Milton. Although he was always talking about my legs and making lewd, geriatric comments, I was able to exploit his interest in me to get my own personal acting training. I initially wrote him a note asking him to speak to me. He came to my house and walked around it looking at my paintings which, as he was a painter himself, gave us something in common. I didn't normally show my paintings to anyone – they were my own private thing – so I was very nervous.

He asked me what I was up to that night and I said I was studying plays. He asked me how it was going and I said I couldn't really understand most of what was going on, so he suggested I take a look at a 1960s Julie Christie classic called Darling. He suggested an actor from the class to work with and said he might come by and watch a rehearsal. He was as good as his word and we ended up rehearsing the piece together, slowly transforming it (and me) into something entirely new.

Being the trooper he was, he wrote and directed me personally in a two-person play, and called it Visions and Lovers. The process took two years and he often hit on me, but I just acted like I was stupid and didn't understand. The rumours about me being cast in Milton's new play were quite an honour, especially since he hadn't done a play for several years. I was the envy of the school; I suddenly became a 'star'. That was when the days of intense scrutiny, which foreshadowed my current private life when I was and still am on TV, began. The play was seventy pages of dialogue and was about a man who was blown away by a beautiful, exotic model who had come into his life.

Milton took the cannon of Darling and transformed it into this play. He created an older, male character who was a brilliant writer; I think it was supposed to be a reflection of him. My character's name was

"She", I kid you not. But "She" was not available to him because of her nymphomaniac tendencies. Oh, sure! What an imagination this man had.

My character was on stage the whole time, which meant I quickly had to get over all my insecurities of being looked at and scrutinised. There is an old adage that actors and models use: "Look at me, look at me, don't look at me". One day Milton showed up to rehearsal with his latest nubile blonde student, Jenna Elfman, who wanted my part. I was terribly freaked out; frightened I would be replaced; afraid they had found out that I was a hack and a no-mark. But whatever his failings, he understood our need to be applauded as artists and he understood the brokenness.

Initially, he was my protector. He saw through the stance, the raised chin and the chip-on-the-shoulder model persona to the insecure, battered young woman that was trying to emerge. One of the things he said to me floored me: "Who would you be if you stopped grinning all the time?" He cottoned on to the fact that I had this funny, smiling façade but that underneath my heart was broken; that I was running around the globe trying to fix it, thinking I had to be perfect.

An old Broadway director turned film director, he would write and rewrite on my narrow shoulders. He taught me stamina and timing and he took me from being frightened of people watching me rehearse to doing the play in front of the six-hundred-strong school, with sell-out performances and encores. And then Milton opened it up to reviewers and the public.

He saw the real me, so I stayed with him until he gave my part – the one I had worked on for two years – to Jenna, whose star was in the ascendant with Dharma and Greg (for which she later won a Golden Globe). That kind of hurt since she was a close 'friend' at the time. We originally bonded at our evening class because we were pretty girls who people assumed couldn't act, so we supported one another. The betrayal slew me, so I had to get away. I was ready then anyway; it was the push I needed to face Hollywood on my own terms.

Milton was a 'Svengali' character for many and, though I'm loath to admit it, he was mine too, albeit without the sex. I was straight up and he knew he was getting nothing like that from me, which was ultimately why he turned on me. On the other hand, Jenna was a very ambitious woman. She promised and suggested more, often walking around the theatre in just a g-string.

In hindsight, I learned a lot from her. She used my friendship and boy was I devoted. I went to her sets when she was starting new jobs and was nervous, because it's nerve-racking to be the new woman on set and some of her early co-stars weren't good to her. But I was on the set of EDTV one day when she gave me a handwritten sealed note to deliver to Milton telling him she wanted my part. Boy was I was naive. Initially, though, his brilliant mind and dazzling focus helped me, piece by piece, to etch out the drama in my soul that had previously been used so negatively and destructively, so that I could start to harness it for good.

I remember Me and Jenna Elfman dancing at her birthday party in LA, where I met Tom Cruise for the first time. Tom Cruise was absolutely hilarious and charming; there's a reason he made it right to the top of the acting business. He was a master with people and knew that he was in a room full of baby actors who were all looking for a break. So when he talked to me he was very self-deprecating and kept repeating my name. He even made a joke about the fact that he didn't cut his hair between films because he never knew who he would be cast as next. He pulled his fringe down to show me that it was on his collarbone, signifying that he hadn't worked in a while either. Considering his power over people and dominance in the industry, I really appreciated the gesture.

TV is a breeze after live theatre. Having carried a whole show and finished my tenure with Milton, I started to work on American TV as a lead actress. Wow! Following in quick succession I guest starred in: Diagnosis Murder, Charmed, Buffy the Vampire Slayer, NYPD Blue, V.I.P., Nip/Tuck, Players and several other hit shows.

I also appeared in a cameo role on How Stella Got Her Groove Back, a romantic film starring Angela Bassett and Taye Diggs. Suzanne Douglas played Stella's sister and had been in the companion piece to the play with me. She was also working with Milton; whatever he did with an actress it bore fruit. Taye was living in NY when he got the part and when he came to LA after the table reading he asked me if I would show him around. He had a girlfriend in NYC and was asking in a purely platonic way, but I never stepped up to the plate because I was too busy with my life at the BHP. Taye went on to do a string of films and was lusted after by most African-American women. I still giggle at my own stupidity, but I'm true to myself. I didn't know what to do with him or where to take him; I'm shyer than people think. I'm more comfortable at home with a group of close friends than in a bar or club, any day.

Milton literally raised my game. For a man in his seventies he was a very difficult man with an ego the size of Hollywood itself. He certainly had issues (don't we all?), but I loved and respected him as my teacher, even though he did some crazy things. He had all his students pay homage to him by standing and applauding whenever he came into the room, even if he'd just been to the toilet. He had certain seats in his ninety-seat theatre roped off in case anyone sat in his teaching seat at the front of the class. What utter madness! If you didn't credit all your success to him he would malign you and start a hate campaign. People were afraid to death of him, so they would join in any criticism he made of you, even if it went against their better judgment. I understood. It was a rather-you-than-me mentality, even if they secretly whispered later they were sorry, or that your work was good. The politics in that place were amazing. Milton explained that the BHP is a microcosm of Hollywood and he was so right about that. Since Hollywood is the biggest fear-based society I have ever experienced, it was excellent training. He was either a pussy cat or a fierce lion; so mercurial you never knew which you would get. After the intense brutality I had experienced at home, Mr Katselas wasn't too terrible for me, it was par for the course. In lieu of protecting me, my mother had always said: "After this you will be able to go anywhere in the world and do anything."

She was right about that. After being a well-respected model and having the keys to the finest things the world had to offer, I recognised that Milton was a bit of a wannabe cad. The way this ridiculous old man was making believe he was king of the film industry when his movies where twenty years old tickled me, but in a strange way it also inspired me. There was something about him: he had nerve and verve. Plus, no matter how many years ago it was, he had been there, and he had conquered.

I reckon he got fatigued by the pressure of sustaining such heights, found drugs and then, as a way out of that, Scientology. He often said: "Don't doubt, just do. Until you get the confidence, borrow mine." There is a saying in Hollywood: "Those that can, do. Those that can't, teach." I find that cruel; teaching is the most underrated profession in the world.

He sent most students off to the Scientology Celebrity Centre and always banged on at me to go, but I was terrified of it. Everyone I knew that got involved with Scientology came out poor financially and changed forever, and not in a healthy way. 'Über actress' Stacy, who at one point would have sold her grandma to be an actress, entered the Celebrity Centre and left as a writer who no longer had any interest in acting. Now that freaked me out.

Milton was a tyrant, but I thank God for him. If you weren't young, beautiful, favoured, supremely talented or on his list you could toil anonymously forever. His master class was filled with people I constantly saw on American TV and all of them credited their success to him. There was a lot of pressure to do so, however. His classes were wonderful and he had a rare gift, so people would agree with whatever he said. They had no choice, he brainwashed everyone to think that they owed everything to him and his students very seldom left, regardless of their accomplishments. It was customary for him to have students for ten or twenty years. I wish I was kidding, but unfortunately I'm not.

BHP was often referred to from the outside as a cult, which it wasn't. I can see why people would say that with its heavy brandishing of Scientology, but that was separate. When people did manage to leave, they would be chased and coaxed back, and if they did leave they would normally do so in anger. Milton would then refer to them as 'blown students', and they would immediately be excommunicated by the masses. But credit where credit is due: he was a visionary, God rest his soul.

As a teacher, he was very confrontational and pushed you beyond your comfort zone. As a result, there were casualties involving people who were unable to take his teaching style and ran around spreading the cult rumour. He didn't suffer fools gladly and nor do I, so I suppose that explains the camaraderie between the two of us. When he critiqued you badly you could cry for days (if you didn't die on the spot!), but when he gave you a golden nugget of suggestion or approval, that was worth thousands of dollars if you followed it.
He called me a banshee, and truthfully I was; in the early days I had as much hope of becoming an actress as becoming the next Queen of England. I had a thick Scouse accent and wasn't patient or studious, nor did I have any track record to suggest I could stay the course. Up until that point I had flitted from one thing to another, one country to another, one job to another. Modelling had suited me because you only had to work one or two days with a client and then you were off to the next. I had a kind of microwave mentality; I was constantly looking for a quick fix.

Acting wasn't it, ultimately, but because it was so hard for me to do, it kept me bound by its challenge. Milton was so unreasonable and so uncomplimentary and the odds were so great, but the voices and negativity from 'them' convinced me that I couldn't quit, if only to prove them wrong.

Milton was what I call a 'frenemy', a friend and an enemy. I loved and hated the man, but in truth I owe him so much. I learned, largely from him, not to let just anyone speak into my artistic life. I have learned the same thing from God when it comes to my spiritual life. The people I allow to speak into my life must have fruit that I admire in theirs. That means they must have a wonderful marriage if they want to talk to me about relationships, or be a marvellous actor or director if they want to give me acting advice. I have learned to tune the others out, although there are many who feel they have the expertise you need: the Church is lined with them.

A few years back I was at a screening for a film I directed, wrote and starred in. Immediately afterwards a young man of about 21, who I had watched do an appalling amateur production at church the week before, said: "Can I tell you something about your acting?" Based on his tone and the calibre of his work, I simply said "no". I know he was shocked, but it had taken me forever to open up. I didn't need some wally closing me down, scoring imaginary points and trying to be cool when he really had nothing to offer.

It's the same with praise. I used to think Milton was mental because he needed so much recognition from people on the one hand, but curiously when they did praise his direction, he never lapped it up, flinched or acted like it had any sway with him. I found that curious. He had Broadway credits and had made seven fabulous Hollywood films giving Richard Gere, Goldie Hawn and Bette Davis his masterful direction. People lined up to work with him and get his confrontational brand of teaching. His classes were hard to get into and very exclusive. In fact Kate Hudson, Goldie's then unknown daughter, was in his class when I was there, as were: Giovanni Ribisi (Avatar), Carlos Bernard (24), Anthony Stewart Head (Buffy the Vampire Slayer) and the list goes on. The actors were either there before they landed jobs that later made them famous, or had had a big hit and were trying to make it back into the limelight. It was a room full of stars. That class was the biggest rush of my life! We were all vulnerable, all waiting for 'papa' to praise us. He taught me the valuable lesson of self-validation, to stamp my own passport as an actor or to declare a piece of art great because that's what I saw. He told me not to wait for the industry, money, jobs, fortune or fame to validate me.

I was working on my Yoga Teacher Training Certificate recently and a volt of electricity that left me paralysed for twenty-four hours passed through my neck. I hadn't even started working out at that point, so I couldn't blame the yoga. Several days later I found out that this was precisely when Milton Katselas passed away! I would have written it off as a coincidence if the same thing hadn't happened to my foot, leaving me lame for twenty-four hours at the time my father passed away. To say Milton had a profound effect on this fatherless girl is a massive understatement.

My big break finally came when I worked with Will Smith in a film called Wild Wild West. It was based on an old television show and I was to be the sexy wench Will had an affair with at the start of the film to cement his sexuality. It paired Will Smith and Barry Sonnenfeld, with whom he had already had a smash hit in Men In Black. Hollywood was desperately rushing to capture the movie gold its top guns felt the duo created, but at this point there wasn't even a script.

No seriously, they didn't have a script! That often happens because the studios are so eager to capitalise on the popularity of a major star, which they see as a magic formula. So often an idea is backed from a pitch without giving it time to develop. Milton was opposed to me taking the part, which was bizarre because, as an acting teacher, he should have wanted his charges to go off into the big wide world and work with the cream of the crop.

He started having his minions page me; I think this was before I owned a cell phone. Instead of congratulating me on the job they expressed nothing but concern. They asked how I would have time to do the part with Will Smith when I was busy working on Milton's play. The play had already been postponed once without warning, and he had subsequently given my role away!

Wild Wild West was doomed from day one. They called me to work a week early, which was very strange. Then Barry Sonnenfeld broke his arm. Barry was a nerd who had become powerful later in life, so he was frightened of me, frightened of my 'sexuality', apparently. Read big mouth, padded bra and fake femme fatale act!

If only he had known I was faking it and was actually quaking in my boots, we would all have been better off. He even told the agency: "She's incredible, but I'm not sure I can handle her." So instead of me being wild, sexy and free I was concerned that I would be too much. I assume that, prior to being in Hollywood where he was a success and women threw themselves at him, he'd had very little experience with women.

Will was more comfortable with comedies than intimate scenes at that time. I'm happy to have seen his film craft develop and that's no longer true, but when he worked with me he was out of his comfort zone. The scene required us to be naked in a massive barrel. He had a sock on his privates (a very big sock!), and I had on nipple tassels and a flesh-coloured G-string! It was meant to be a closed set but we had all kind of visitors. Naughty Kevin Kline was hilarious, he kept freaking me out by threatening to come and watch me 'work'.

Jada Pinket Smith was on set all the time. Now that's amazing because we were doing night shoots and she was in the latter stages of pregnancy with Jaden, so to say she stands by her man is an understatement. But this made it hard for me and Will to do what we needed to do for the screen liaison to look real. So instead of the hot passionate Wild Wild West opening the producers had envisioned, we just simmered. So instead of Wild Wild West, we were more of a lame tame mess that fizzled out.

A film takes about a year to come out, so I had no idea that I was no longer in the film until I went to visit Will on the set of the MTV awards just before it was due to be released. He's a nice man and was very considerate when we were working together. We both had to be constantly sprayed with water and his was warmed to a specific temperature but mine wasn't. When he saw me shuddering with the shock of being blasted he had a word with someone and they heated mine too.

But at the awards he was acting really strangely. I couldn't understand what was bothering him, but then his makeup artist Pearce pulled me to one side and said: "You didn't make the cut. They reshot your part with another actress, Garcelle Beauvais." Garcelle was a lovely girl who, like me, had made the successful transition from model to actress. I knew her because you generally know who is in your 'category'.

She knew Will from his Fresh Prince of Bel-Air days. To this day I have no problem with her, which is interesting. I guess I knew she had nothing to do with the decision. It was more to do with Barry Sonnenfeld and his partner Barry Josephson; actresses at that level have no control. She never went after the part like Jenna Elfman did with the play. Jenna was willing to lose my friendship and snap me in two, but Garcelle merely stepped in when things were revised. It happens daily in Hollywood, but it had never happened to me. I was horrified. Will had told me on sight that I was "a star", and he meant it. He was incredibly kind and gracious to me, so what had happened?

I was reeling, embarrassed, distraught and horrified. I had told the world and his wife that I was going to be in this film. It had a major bankable movie star in it, and was overseen by a major director at that time in Hollywood, so being linked on screen with Will Smith had the power to cement my career. When agents heard I had been cast I moved up the ladder even before I got on set. But there is something terribly out of balance when you need a part because without it you feel worthless. Somewhere while I was toiling in Hollywood I had lost perspective. I didn't have family to ballast me so I had no centre.

I had given up too much normality to be in LA: birthdays, weekends, holidays and family vacations had all been missed, so I felt I needed a big payoff. I was in trouble but I didn't realise how badly. I began to shake apart. All the external things I had done to make it seemed to have failed and I began to feel really miserable. All the pain I had run from was back to get me.

Failure is hard to shake. There's an odour to failure; it's pervasive and as clingy as the smell of an old, dank bar; the rotten smell of rubbish in the heat. You can't quite shake it off and you convince yourself that everybody else can smell it too. I sank. For the first time in my life I didn't know how to fix this one. I didn't have the heart or the energy, and worse still, I didn't care to. I cried so much I thought I would die; I was completely humiliated.

I planned to kill myself and was going to do it by putting the gas on because the pain I carried inside and this new humiliation made me feel like all my brother's pronouncements had come true. There just wasn't enough alcohol to numb it. I still didn't know that the hole in my soul couldn't be filled with these acting roles, magazines covers, or flirting with boys – my three favourite things. Suddenly there it was: the epiphany that it wasn't my mother's, my errant father's or my brother's fault. At some point you become a grown up and have to start taking some responsibility, acknowledging that it's not about the colour you were born or the financial level you came in at.

The only thing worse than abject failure is sitting in poverty having walked away from the bright lights of modelling to gamble on becoming an actor. I actually spent more time walking people's dogs and babysitting their children! I was fed up, I can tell you. I felt like I was washed up, that all the luck I had found or drummed up had wasted away through my poor choices, because I couldn't be satisfied with the modelling story I had created for myself. I felt as though my greed had blown up in my face. Alcoholics Anonymous have a saying: "poor me, poor me, pour me another drink" and I realise now that the pity party I threw was a total waste of time, but it was my only strategy back then when things didn't go my way.

I owned a naughty American pit bull called Calvin. He was possessive and jealous and loved me in a crazy way. I loved that critter because his reaction to me was the same whether I was on the cover of a magazine (a rarity at that time in my life), or in a hit play (sadly also a rarity). He was a strange one. He was a beautiful tan colour, but had a split nose which made him unique. He was from show stock, but the nose prevented him from being shown on the pedigree circuit. I felt that something was messing with my own pedigree, so perhaps I empathised with him more than was healthy. He was the type of beast that attracted lots of attention but could seldom handle it, just like me. He just ran off when the attention got too much for him.

But there was no need for Calvin to die with me, so I started thinking about how to get him out of the house. I lived too near Sunset Boulevard to let him out, so I felt that if he did go – which, knowing his loyalty to me he wouldn't – he would get killed immediately by a juggernaut (it had to be something big and dramatic, I'm not an actress for nothing!). But if he stayed in the house with me he would die. Now that's not fair. I was also a little tipsy at the time, so thinking all this through was difficult. In any case, I didn't turn the gas on, I stopped drinking instead. I was so scared by this incident that I didn't touch alcohol for four years afterwards.

I gamely joined Alcoholics Anonymous, not because I was an alcoholic but because I came from stock that had been riddled with the problem. I wanted to learn from people who had decided to stop drinking, and the Twelve-Step Programme was great therapy. It was time to look into the things that held me down and got in my way, whether real or imagined, and I had a blast. There was a meeting at noon on the Sunset Strip in West Hollywood at a coffee house, imaginatively named "The Coffee House", which later moved next door to Dublin's Irish Pub.

The place had twenty seats and you could only reserve one fifteen minutes before the meeting. Janice Dickenson was there, as was Robert Downey Junior and Anthony Kedis from the Red Hot Chilli peppers. It was a group of really creative people and we were all survivors of something; a gorgeous group of souls, abounding in talent and beauty, but mired by something.

The alcohol was the least of it; we all wanted our lives to improve. I really loved the conversations in there, which I would never share. The only reason I named the few I did is because they have written about their own struggles to move past these issues themselves. Many people who now populate our screens were there, but I would never tell on them.

I self-graduated from AA after four years because after studying alcoholics for that length of time I knew I wasn't one. But the information gleaned from that period of sobriety was really incredible. I would challenge anyone to try it. It's also amazing how much more I got done, and how much freer and more fun my life became. It was a challenge but, like anyone I suppose, I had a tendency to lean on alcohol when I was stressed or had a shocking disappointment, or when I was bored at one of the many functions actors get invited to. That was the time Step Two of the programme started to shape me. This stage marks the point at which we: "Came to believe that a Power greater than ourselves could restore us to sanity".

I had hit a wall financially, as this was the first period since I was about twenty that my career wasn't paying for itself. I had never had a support job since the one in The Grosvenor all those years before. I decided to rent out my house and go live with someone to reduce costs. I asked my sister who lived in South Central LA with her husband, but she wouldn't give me the time of day, so I called my friend James and asked him if I could move into his place. I was used to his benevolence as he often had people stay with him for long periods while we were at acting school. I hadn't spoken to him for about a year after we had survived our tyrannical, often abusive acting school. But as mutual survivors of Milton Katselas we shared an unbreakable bond. True to form, and without hesitation, he said: "Yes, do you want to move in tonight, rent free?" What a star!
He even came round with a friend to move the big items out of the house, but for some reason I put him off, pretending I had found a housemate. I loved my West Hollywood cottage and had been determined to live in it until I became a star, so moving out because I couldn't afford it, and admitting that the big Hollywood dream hadn't

happened for me, was not part of my plan. James didn't look too wonderful himself at the time; he had gained forty pounds, and had a dead look in his eyes.

This was Jamie boy, our class star and the finest actor I had ever met. He was an intelligent, witty man of integrity and had acted since he was ten. He had bought numerous properties and yet Hollywood was so hard on him. At that time he had given up, pretending that he didn't want to act anymore. We all do that, it's a mechanism I am very familiar with to say you have quit rather than admit that the industry doesn't want you. The business thrives on named talent, so if you are a talent with no name value, it's harder and harder to break in or stay in – no matter how good you are. Once you get there, role size dwindles and your experience starts to count for nothing. Added to this, you have no work experience outside of acting, so you can't get any other job. It's a tough negotiation unless you are very young, very beautiful or have a benefactor that can open a door or two.

I had been offered many of those: rich, successful actors, agents and producers who wanted a hot girl on their arm in exchange for a helping hand up the ladder, but no thank you. I have had 'producers' call my agent, set up a meeting with me and then chase me around the room. When I finally decide to give up the whole notion of acting, I am going to tell all, to have a role call; a name it and shame it moment. I can't wait! But for now I have to be prudent, so suffice to say I'm an actress not a whore. I didn't want a benefactor or pimp and Jamie didn't have them either. He was actually going from casino to casino gambling. I didn't know any of this at first, but like all good sagas it was revealed in the fullness of time. I just knew that my old friend was missing in action.

About a week later, after using all the avoidance tactics in the world, I had to face the truth. It hadn't happened for me. I called James again, ready to let go of my fantasy life and he was still as enthused as he had been the week before. There was one rule though: so familiar was he with Calvin and his bad behaviour, that he stipulated no dogs!!!

Calvin and Millie, my other dog, another triangle But I had realised that a group of three doesn't have to be so terrifying if you are with the right beings (human or not). These two were amazing; they don't call them man's best friend for nothing. They really were a healing balm. I was desperate about not being able to take them, but I was also newly sober, lonely, financially wrecked and in need of support. I had nowhere else to turn, so I looked for a new home for the two of them. Millie was sweet and was adopted straight away, but Calvin's reputation preceded him: Californians are not as brave as the English. A pit bull on the streets I was raised on in England was a trophy or, bizarrely, some kind of family dog. I came to learn that this was not so in Cali. They were demonised, denoting gangster rappers and crime. Whatever! He was supposed to go to a pit bull rescue centre from the pound in Santa Monica but he had a fight with another dog and fatally wounded it, so they put him down. No amount of tears, angry fist-shaking or looking for a scapegoat to blame brought that boy back, though I tried all of it. At the time, Calvin and Millie were my family. I love dogs and children for their guilelessness.

Chapter Ten: My Redeemer

> London
>
> 7 countries (Amsterdam, Sweden, Rome, Paris, Madrid, London & Germany) in 15 days and 4 more days to go in L.A. for the Grammys
>
> Talk to you soon
>
> Roxanna
>
> Phirin Orache
> 1148 S. Sherbourne Dr.
> #5
> Los Angeles CA.
> 90035 U.S.A.

I got a postcard from Roxanna when I was bumming around in Hollywood. I was broke and the acting dream had ceased to work for me. The only person who had stayed in touch from that glorious time in NYC, which at this point felt like a dream of yesteryear – was my friend Roxanna, the big sister I had always wanted. She gave me instruction, wisdom and support, even backing me when I made mistakes (and what twenty-three-year-old girl doesn't make them?!)

She was honest and caring enough to express her concern about me because she felt dark-skinned didn't tend to make it in the acting business the same way girls with lighter skin did. I didn't buy into that, but she had felt that I was doing brilliantly as a model and should stay put. I went anyway, but she never let go of me. She was always better than me at keeping in touch with people; she kept up with me no matter where she was in the globe, or who she was with. She was loyal, profound and had an incredible sense of humour. She was hilarious and had an ability to go far beyond skin deep.

The most amazing part of her legacy was that she was just normal. To her credit, she stayed loyal and grounded no matter what her situation was. She told me she still wanted to know me even though I had fallen flat on my face. Ouch! That postcard was hard to receive because she meant well, but it made me feel that if I hadn't chased dreams and been greedy at least I would have been making money as a model.

When I was broke and my world had collapsed, she invited me to NYC. We worked together on a magazine cover and she shared a secret with me. I had watched her excel for years and thought it was largely due to her solid family background. She was an only child, so she had no messes with her siblings, but she told me her success came through her relationship with Christ! What? I didn't know what she was talking about. A relationship? How can you have a relationship with a man that had been dead for more than two thousand years? She was playing a song that I had never heard before, but that was somehow familiar to me. "No weapon formed against me shall prosper," the singer crooned over and over again. As I walked around NYC that day, I couldn't get those words out of my mind.

I briefly tried to go back to modelling because the acting game seemed too tough. I didn't see it at the time because I was only in NYC for a few days, but I managed to get on the cover of Heart and Soul magazine. Roxanna did the makeup and Mark Baptiste, one of New York's finest black photographers, created the magic. I loved working with him, he had so much energy. Two years later this cover was on the wall of Duke's Coffee Shop, my favourite diner. As a result, a casting director looked for me and I got a role in The Forsaken, a film I really enjoyed making.

Roxanna was wonderful. She gave me a tape and a Bible, and I was never the same again. It was Roxanna who led me to faith in Christ. She discipled me long-distance from NYC to LA, sending me teaching tapes from various ministers: TD Jakes from The Potter's House in Dallas; and my favourite, Joyce Meyer, a lovely minister from Fenton, Missouri. She says: "Hurt people hurt people", and she should know. She was abused sexually by her father from the age of thirteen, leading her into a marriage that was dysfunctional and doomed. She had basically married the first man that asked her, so low was her self-esteem. Joyce was the perfect woman to minister to me because I could relate to her wounds. She's also very candid about her roughness, her harsh speaking voice and her harsher still – and overly emotional – personality, check, check, check! But by the grace and power of God and the biblical lessons learned, she now has a very strong second marriage that has lasted more than thirty years. I was impressed with her ministry and her life. So she, along with other influences, started me thinking about God. Through his grace and power I knew I was able to stop the cycle of alcoholism and misery I saw around me that was perpetuating itself in my life. One day at a time, choice by choice. Left to my own devices I could have drunk and shagged myself to death.

What's wrong with that? I hear you cry. Why not, huh? Because I tried it, and I always came up empty. It's not God's best; it was never God's plan for my life. As James said to me once when I was in a rotten, misery-inducing, sexed up, co-dependent relationship, when all we did was shag and shout: "Shagging can be a priority, but it can't be your first priority".

I had to realise that I was repeating the horrid patterns I had witnessed growing up. I figured there was a victim and there was an abuser. My father had battered and victimised my mother while we were little girls, which is possibly why she was numb to the pain I suffered at my brother's hand. I decided back then that I wasn't going to play that role. Instead I would be the 'love them and leave them', non-committal type; that way I couldn't get hurt. It seemed to me that being emotionally vulnerable was the key to misery.

Indeed, since I am a woman, the devilish double standard exists: if I sleep around with abandon I'm a slag, a slut, a whore; I am unwifely material. It ticks me off, but it probably saved my life. I'm not constrained by these rules, I'm liberated by them. If I had my own way, I wouldn't do rules, I wouldn't even have morals. But then the ugliness I was freed from by accepting God's ways wouldn't work.

That's the way my alter ego, Liberty Baker, from Footballers' Wives was. In that sense she seems like a liberated character, right? I don't think so. If that series had carried on or if I had lived that way, full of drugs and deceit, she and I would have been on our way down. I really wanted to be a bad girl when I was a young woman; it looked like so much fun. And maybe it is for a season, but bad girls end up in bad places.

That's not always true for boys in the short term. They seem to get away with it as our culture views the man who can't stay faithful, the one who puts it about, as a bit of a hero (insert the name of a Premier League footballer/star golfer here). These men are seen as studs, but I can tell you that it catches up with them, even if it takes a lifetime. Try hanging out with a former bad boy when he's reached his fifties or sixties. The publicist sells it well, but the man who has repeatedly cheated and lost the respect of his wife and first set of kids always has moments of quiet desperation that he wouldn't dare tell the masses about. Trust me, he is now on his third or fourth wife wondering where it all went wrong.

There is a double standard and then there's God's standard. The double standard is that men can bed a thousand women and still be a catch. Men can sneak off and employ women to have sex with them and not get persecuted even when the woman does: by the courts and by society. They generally don't marry that type of girl; they may play with them all day, but they won't take them home to their mothers or introduce them to their mates. That's why so many desperate girls are kissing and telling on footballers and rock stars. They get angry when the man treats them poorly after they have had sex, but these chicks need to pull up their knickers and have some self-respect.

Look at Marilyn Monroe. Her beauty was lost to us forever once the drugs, booze and promiscuous lifestyle took their toll on her. Look at some of the 'it' girls we have for our girls to look up to. Some very high-profile young actresses and singers have imploded in front of us in recent years: shaving their heads and passing out drunk in front of the paparazzi; going to jail; getting fired from movie sets. Every teenage girl used to want to be them, but who does now?

God's standard is that sex is a wonderful, God-given thing, but He wants us to be in a committed marital relationship to enjoy it. His plan isn't to spoil our fun, it's to prevent the heartache of being used and unloved, of creating children you can't support, of preventing a lot of pain.

A different level of intimacy is reached when a man and a woman spend time really getting to know one another and don't just jump each other's bones. I wasn't interested in this teaching and I certainly wasn't interested in putting it to the test. I got a lot of validation from being a sexy woman and scarcely had clothes that covered my body, so the idea of not sleeping with my boyfriend or anyone else until I met my husband was terrifying to me. I thought Christians were nuts! So I embraced most of the Bible but left that part alone. Thank you very much.

Chapter Eleven: Finding my family

I began a journey of awakening and started to really study the Bible and get grounded. I understood for the first time that I was a human being, not a human doing, and that I was still ok if I wasn't 'achieving' every minute. This was a new concept for me! Before this, if someone had asked me how I was doing, I would have listed my latest three accomplishments; I must have been unbearable to know.

I also learned to trust and rely on women rather than constantly looking for men to help and validate me as I had in the past. I had a wonderful teacher in my pastor, Regina, who was a beautiful Mexican bombshell. She was in her fifties, although you would never know that when you see her in her tight-fitting jeans and cowboy boots. She was strong and classy and had an inner strength and wisdom that I have never known. Regina had a strong marriage and was like Roxanna: there was something different about both of these women. She and her husband led the alcoholic recovery ministry in our little church, so it was the perfect place for me to be discipled. I got a great chance to understand recovery from a Christian perspective while learning firsthand about the ways of God. I got into a prayer habit that I still have now, and also formed key relationships with women for the first time, which I still uphold, even across long distances. In short, I got myself several new sisters.

My life is proof that "God uses the weak and the foolish things of the world to confound the wise" (1 Corinthians 1:27).

There had been a powerfully destructive work in my family before I was born, but our household was in denial, which is the worst approach because you don't know what you're up against if no one will admit there's a problem. My mother can't even think about what she unwittingly allowed to happen to her baby girls. Nothing that I experienced even comes close to what my sister who survived the fire lives through on a daily basis.

Many people asked me over the years: "You're so pretty, why aren't you married?" I'm only just coming to terms with the answer. My mother was so weakened by my dad's drinking, dysfunction and desertion that I was wary. He was so proud of his son and gave him real preference; he dressed my brother in three-piece suits. He wouldn't allow anyone but him to sit in the front seat of the car, relegating his wife and three daughters to the back seat. This was his way of saying that women should take the backseat and men should lead.

So the only marriage I witnessed was so devastating to the females – the wife and in turn the daughters – I naturally avoided it like the plague. I had to do several rounds with Jesus before I could allow a man to get to know me. Regina was the first lady I could relate to who spoke to me about the Lord. Although I had been listening to Joyce for a while, I needed someone who I could actually see living their life. Honey, I know PR; I needed to see someone live it.

Regina had a healthy marriage and was passionate and openhearted. I always thought Christian women had to wear tan nylon tights, pearls and a twinset, with eighties, Dallas-style wings at the sides of their hair. So when this sexy, fashionably dressed woman with long, raven-coloured hair approached me I was pleasantly surprised.

She came to talk to me at the insistence of a man, J, who I had followed into the church. I went after seeing him at a beach AA meeting, so I didn't actually go there to find Jesus. This guy suggested I speak to Regina because he really liked me, but he could tell I was hard work. It takes one to know one, right? J became a good friend as he was as broken by his life and family as I was. But God knew the only way to get me into church was to send a little cutie in first!

Denial is amazing. I had no idea what had driven me to model, to act or to look for male validation. I didn't even realise I was looking for validation. The first thing Regina told me was that I was immature, based on the way I looked and the 'refinements' I had gained from the industry. Despite being a thirty-year-old woman, I came across as a scrappy teenager.

I think this is because my mother couldn't school me in the things she didn't know herself. On top of that were my own wounds and an unacknowledged date rape. We had been taught to carry on, but at that point I couldn't. I had a history of chronic physical and mental abuse at the hands of my brother and a broken heart because the entertainment industry hadn't 'fixed me' by giving me the huge film I had naively hoped would make me a success.

Regina spent about two years giving me (and other women like me) intense discipleship and counselling, and she did it for free. She was compelled to do it, because another woman had done the same to help her heal from the mess she had grown up in. What a godly woman she is; what an encourager of my soul. She started the process with prayer and an announcement that at some point she would fail me, largely because she was human. But she assured me that Jesus never would.

She focused her ministry on prostitutes, women who had done prison time, women who had lost their kids and women with alcoholism. I went to group and private sessions with her to look at my own depression and its connection to alcohol. It was amazing that I'd spent all this time trying to be someone big and I found myself with people that nobody wanted: the misfits, the people the world we live in would term losers, the ugly, the dirty, the poor and the broken. I had the best time of my life listening to the heart of people who had nothing to lose, who had surrendered fully because they didn't have a choice. This was truly the lap of greatness because everywhere else I went people had their masks on. They hid behind the designer clothes, the beautiful makeovers and the hangovers from the drink or drugs used to take the edge off the pressures of living in the twenty-first century.

Regina told me that in households where there was denial of abuse, the people who live alongside you are normally unable to help you, to have empathy for you. They certainly never offer loyalty because they're too busy surviving themselves. That made sense. My mother couldn't protect my sister from the flames because she was busy protecting her skull from my father's boot. She couldn't protect me from the humiliating, soul-destroying beatings I received before I left home. In fact she actually left me in a situation that was so terrifying I had to get up and get the hell out of there. She always put her needs before other people's and she always will. That doesn't make her a bad person, just a broken one. I had to work at forgiving her then and I still do daily. Otherwise I drag her on every voyage I take, whether it's good or bad, and thus render myself useless because I'm weighed down with the baggage. I forgave my brother years ago; I see him as a victim like me and my sisters. He has done so many things to hurt himself that if I had a vengeful spirit against him, which I don't, I could say that he already got his just deserts. But I don't feel like that... I love him too much. That alone confirms to me that the Lord has changed me, because I wanted him dead during the toughest periods of violence.

When I help him or spend time with him now it's really difficult; there are so much unspoken horrors and I'm still very frightened of him. I don't think he would lay a finger on me, but the irrational fear persists. However, he often needs so much help I have to lay it to one side. We're survivors of the same war. I have two birth sisters and quite a few supernatural sisters: Vera, Roxanna, Jody, Donna, Gayle, Frances and Mother Regina. I always fight with my birth sisters because of the jealousy and madness we experienced, but I have found the supernatural ones as I have gone through life. These new sisters have shown me it's OK to be who I am without having to deal with all the insecurity, blame, misunderstanding and darkness that sometimes come from my birth sisters.

I take love and support from whoever gives it freely. First Christ and then the girls He has sent as friends, mentors and teachers; I have been blessed with many. I truly believe that God sent me them to heal me, and that I, in turn, can help heal the girls coming up behind me. Before I became a mother, I was a big sister in the Big Sisters of Greater Los Angeles programme, which was a wonderful opportunity to help out a young girl. Mine was called Princess and she was brilliant. She helped me see how far I had come and she reminded me of myself at ten. She lapped up whatever I gave her; I have never been to Disneyland as many times as I did when I was that child's big sister.

It can be such a love/hate thing with my birth sisters. On a good day they back me more strongly than anyone else and would never let anyone mistreat me, but on a bad day it's anyone's guess. For a while there was nothing but bad days but then, out of nowhere, it turned and we enjoyed a season of calm and consideration. I have learned not to delve into the drama that starts the cycle. It would either make you laugh or cry to see how fragile these relationships are.

One of my sisters makes me laugh more than anyone else on the planet. She is naughty, outrageous and bodacious, but she can also be vicious when you impose a boundary, or when she feels threatened – which is often when she's with me. She is nomadic and wild, which I admire until it hurts me. I see her sporadically, fall in love with her, get hurt by her, fall out of love with her and try to save her from her husband and her own choices.

I sometimes have to close my heart and move on. I admire her because she has the tenacity (or the foolishness) to back someone who has let her down so spectacularly, time after time. But I don't believe love should be so painful. I could see her mirroring the alcoholic co-dependent relationship we saw as girls and immediately warned her off him, but it caused blue murder so now I leave her to her own dealings, but I always try to be compassionate.

On the plus side, she is my prayer partner and a real entrepreneur, who has kept me on my toes in goal setting and accomplishments, but more seriously in matters of the Spirit. She was the leader in all things God-related as she became a Christian first. I thought she was just having a moment and I remember having to be dragged to her baptism, holding down the mirth I felt. At the time I thought that if anyone was an unlikely candidate to become a Christian, she was it.

The same can be said now of me; however, I started laughing on the other side of my face when I saw how much God had changed her.

She is still wild and still always has more than one colour running through her hair, but all that divine, creative madness that made her life a mess got focused. She went from being a person with lots of ideas to an executer of them and a winner, and then she became generous! Our kid? Well if that wasn't a miracle in itself then I don't know what is!

It was ultimately short-lived as she backslid, which many Christians do from time to time, and now and again she exhibited at lot of her angry, nasty behaviour again, throwing in a Bible verse or two when it suited her. Then she regained her faith – it is after all a battle – and this time it lasted long enough to convince me that there was something in it for me to check out and explore.

The other significant thing for me was that she was able to maintain her fiery individuality and her fabulous dress sense, which challenged me because I thought being a Christian meant you had to be bland, sexless and compliant. I am none of these things and nor are the legions of people who have offered me a helping hand!

I am getting to know my other natural sister again as we spent many years apart when I was living in the States. She is the oldest, so she witnessed a lot more of our parents' dysfunction than I did. She's also a sensitive soul, so often you hurt her without even being aware of it; it's very, very tiresome. She is scarred by our parents, as we all are, and I really love her, but it's a balancing act. When I first came home she was always complaining about my mother's affection for me, and where that left her, which was naturally uncomfortable for me. What could I say to that even if I thought it was valid? I have learned to live without both of them because often I have had to. Although I enjoy it immensely when we get along, I just can't count on it.

Spiritually I trust Roxanna and Regina, obviously, but on a daily basis I talk with Jody, Bertha and, on occasion, Vera. Coincidentally they are all brown girls. They are all prayer warriors and all tell me the truth, kindly! They're not afraid to admire my inner life and my spiritual gifting, while also being really clear about my madness, my strong-willed behaviour and my temper. They are all kinder to me than I am to myself and each prays for me daily as I do for them; sometimes with me, sometimes in my absence.

That's a new thing for me, a healing thing. Since I got involved with Pastor Regina and the church I have learned to see women as friends rather than enemies. I am no longer competing for the scarce eligible male, or for attention. Obviously my upbringing and the fashion industry left several wounds that the acting industry would have continued to rub salt into had I not had some sort of (for want of a better way of putting it) "divine intervention".

Now let's be clear, if anybody who knew me fifteen years ago heard me banging on about Scripture and God they would yell "hypocrite" or "mad woman". I had a mouth like a sewer and never had clothes that fully covered my body. I would knock you out in a fight if I had to and I used to need people to like me, so I was very adept at saying what I thought they wanted to hear. None of this made me a great witness.

I probably would have been one of the first to say I was blagging or that this was a phase, but the 'phase' has continued and has borne much fruit. Never in my wildest dreams did I ever think I would believe in God, go to church or become celibate, which I was for the two-and-a-half years before I met my husband. Nor did I think I would ever try to live in a way that didn't serve me and my appetites first. I don't always succeed, but I feel better for the battle. The nightmares I lived through at home have been refined by a harvest of characters that have liberated my soul one by one.

Chapter Twelve: Famine strikes

During that period I had renewed grace within the acting industry and got booked for every job I auditioned for. It was an incredible period, but it only lasted about a year and then the opposite happened. I suddenly couldn't get a job to save my life. I was learning firsthand that God is neither a magician nor my genie in a bottle. He doesn't just sit around in heaven waiting to fix everything for us.

Ultimately I had to deal with life on life's terms and to realise that faith does not protect you from hard times. That change of perspective gave me strength. My fight with God continued all through that year and I was continually tempted to go back to doing things my way. I was constantly looking for boys to distract me and trying to scam my way back to glory in true Oruche fashion.

I had the pleasure of getting to know Robert De Niro while he was shooting ill-fated film Showtime. We met on an aeroplane when I was coming back from a press junket for my film, The Forsaken, and he was heading back to work after flying home for the weekend. I guess we were placed together because we were both paid for by the Hollywood studios. I was tipped off by one of the flight attendants that Mr De Niro would be seated next to me; never has a makeup brush been dragged across my face with such speed and precision! If he had just shown up I would have fainted, but as it was I was able to get all the bravado in the world together. But what a shy man! The heavy New York accent he often uses for his parts is definitely not him, the real De Niro is such a contradiction to his "Are you talkin' to me?" gangster persona, or to the Jake LaMotta (Raging Bull) or Travis Bickle (Taxi Driver) characters we have all come to know and love.

He was soft-spoken and insisted that I call him "Bob", which seemed funny since he's such a legend. It was odd to be on such intimate terms with an actor of that stature. You could have knocked me over with a feather! When he put his luggage in the overhead bins I said: "I've got a laptop up there: break it and you'll have to pay." Oh he loved that, since everybody else kissed his derrière and literally wouldn't leave him alone.

After that first chance meeting we met up on a couple of other occasions and whenever he took me to dinner the owners closed the restaurant. It was kind of fabulous and kind of creepy, but he was a real laugh. He underplays his incredible power with self-deprecating humour, which is probably the best way to deal with it. The guy probably doesn't have normal conversations very often, because you are so aware of what he has created that even if you don't think you're reacting to it, you can't help it.

Waiters buzzed around us like flies, dying to fulfil to his every whim. Glasses were topped up after every sip, and while I was sitting with him I realised that the wonderful work I was courting – which I had thought I wanted and that brings the world to your feet – comes with a hefty price tag.

Just to get my goat, my Mercedes was off-limits because it needed to be repaired and I didn't have the money. I was driving an awful borrowed car at the time, which reflected my fortunes; it was a white, late-eighties Nissan. Oh the horror! My ego was in bits about it, which is my fault for buying into the whole image madness in the first place. He was like: "I'm a New Yorker; I don't give a shit about that kind of shit." He was very naughty and powerful and was used to having things his own way. I learned a lot from him.

He was super-focused, getting up at four in the morning to work out, then working sixteen hours on set, then on to a production meeting for the next project with his film company Tribeca Films. He was always looking ahead. This was a man in his sixties, who knows this business better than anyone. He initially wanted to get in my knickers: his marriage was breaking down with Grace Hightower and he was lonely.

I was intrigued, but there is a thirty-year age gap that no amount of acting gold could bridge, plus he is world-famous for picking up black women. I wasn't even sure he was seeing the real me, I think I was just his type. I still believe I have more to offer than making it by visiting a famous man's groin, but it was a test at the time since I was itching to make my next film and a call from him on my behalf could have changed my destiny. But I didn't want to make it like that. We had dinner a bunch of times and he pursued me with a vengeance until he realised that I was not on the menu and he never called again. But before he took off he gave me the number for an acting coach he uses, who told me to go directly to the Actors Studio in Manhattan.

How can you ignore an acting suggestion from Robert De Niro? I'm certainly not that arrogant! I decided to take my destiny into my own hands and retrained because I had lost my confidence. It doesn't take long for that to happen when you're auditioning constantly and not booking anything. I became a lifelong member of the Actors Studio after auditioning for two years!

I then went on to study in the Directors' Programme and turned my back on Hollywood in the conventional sense. I began writing, directing and producing my own scripts and hiring the multitude of actors that I saw waiting around for their big break. I was finally happy; I felt like I had been released from my box; freed from waiting to be called to work. Probably the hardest thing about acting is that someone else decides when you get to do it. I suppose it's the same for all lines of work, but with acting it's the shortness of the contracts that makes you feel powerless, and unemployment is a big part of the game initially.

Then I got a call from an agent I had hooked up with in London three years earlier. I didn't actually want to go back to London as I had dark memories there that I wasn't ready to face. I didn't like the weather and I also didn't relish starting over and making new friends again after turning thirty. Worse than that, I would be forced to live with my mother and open myself up to her insanity again.

I had finished film school and had just screened my directorial debut film Selah at the oldest theatre in Hollywood, the Egyptian Theater, which is right next to the shrine auditorium where they now hold the Oscars. That was a buzz. I was cutting a documentary using my new editing tools, which made me happy. On the other hand, right after screening my film I was made homeless.

The timing was curious. I was staying way out in the San Fernando Valley and my house had been sold from under me by a greedy neighbour turned property developer, Keith, who had previously conned one of my elderly neighbours out of her property in a scandalous way. I found out when I came out of my front door to find a man taking measurements for something or other. I really didn't want to leave my little house at the top of Sunset Boulevard with its massive garden, where I lived for practically nothing. I had even planned to buy the cottage, although it was proving to be financially out of my league. It was actually the guest house of another property and although the lots were separated by fencing, they were were worth well over a million dollars.

The cottage was ramshackle at best, but it was prime real estate on the corner of Sunset and San Vicente Boulevards. Behind it were famous venues such as The Viper Room, Billboard Live (now Key Club), The Roxy Theater, Whisky A Go Go ("The Whisky") and my favourite breakfast spot, Duke's.

Around this time, my dog Eloise, a French bulldog, was stolen from the yard. This is poignant because I would never have left her behind after what happened to the other dogs. I was really comfortable there; I loved that little cottage and had decided to live there forever. But this approach tends to be a problem as I take my most ardent creative strides when circumstances push me. All of a sudden, the things that had bound me to LA were gone.

My friend Marty kindly put me up and kept all my furniture in his garage. But even though I was now in just one room, the idea of flying to London for an audition just wasn't on the cards. I was emboldened by my new hat as director, editor and writer; I didn't want to subject myself to the harsh side of the business again. My

London agent Pierre knew exactly what to say. He asked me how my LA agent was working out and I confessed that I didn't really have one, or a home for that matter. So the cheeky git said: "No chance of work, then." He knows an actor's hunger. I told him to send me the pages and he sent me three.

The character was wonderful: a model, a diva, a bisexual drug addict and an angry woman who used her body to manipulate and cheat. What a part! I knew I was going to get the role as soon as I read it. Nobody ever gets models right because the women who play them have a fantasy idea about the lifestyle. The women generally don't look like models even if they are pretty because models have a certain look; they're not even necessarily pretty, in actual fact.

I got on the internet and booked a ticket, which cost me $1,300. This was to be my big break, my ambition to be an actor had come out of the deep freeze it had been relegated to. I told everybody but James that I had the part already; no one understands the madness of what you have to go through for this profession. No one gets why you would make that kind of sacrifice except a kindred spirit. I also decided that if I didn't get it I would fake my own death (I'm kidding). I sold my household belongings and my brand new car, threw a party and headed off to London.

Chapter Thirteen: Be careful what you wish for, you just might get it

I arrived at Gatwick Airport on June 26, 2005. I couldn't believe it had been fourteen years since I had been "home". During my time in Los Angeles (with a little bit of New York sprinkled in for bad behaviour) I had been shocked at the madness and realness of all the immigrants and illegal taxi drivers asking me if I wanted a ride. I had forgotten how multicultural Britain was, or maybe it wasn't like that when I left.

I was saddled with bags and looked like I was travelling to Mecca or Lourdes. In a way I was, because I had every earthly possession with me: computers, dresses, wigs, makeup, and of course my Blackberry. This was an opportunity I couldn't pass up; it was the key to a new life. Footballers' Wives was the big one, and I was here to stake my claim.

I was tired and bewildered, and I felt like I was in Ghana or New Delhi. LA was blond, bland and whitewashed; even the black girls looked like white girls dipped in chocolate over there. But in LA one of my wonderful friends, usually Jamie boy, would have already been there waiting for me in a Ford pickup truck, a cup of Starbucks on the dashboard, sunglasses on, the radio pumping and screaming, "Girl I missed you!" And that was after I'd only been gone ten days.

I had called ahead to announce the exciting news of my arrival and it was agreed that one of them would be there to meet me since there were five adults in the London area who could have come. So I was surprised that there was no one there to welcome me! I called my sister after waiting in bewilderment and said: "Is anybody here to pick me up?" She snarled: "Why the @"£$ are you asking me?" I could pretend to have said: "Because I'm your sister", but I've had five years to think of a rebuttal line and it's not even a great one.

I was starting to feel jetlagged, culturally shocked and disappointed. But why did I expect her to pick me up after all the craziness in our relationship? In part because I love all of them deeply and hoped one day they would be able to show me some love too. I had bags everywhere and the taxi drivers were circling around me like vultures. I managed to prop my bags up and call my mother's house. I supposed that, as usual, she would be late or driving the wrong way down a dual carriage way causing havoc.

To my chagrin she answered the phone: "Oh Phi love, erm, I'm supposed to be at work but the schedule changed. I did remember... Shall I come now?" I wanted to scream: "Where is my welcome, I've been gone half my life!" My mother drives at thirty mph at the best of times. I'm a big girl so, though disappointed, I said: "Don't worry about it mum, I'll get a cab." Now that got her attention. My mother said "What?! Give the money to me! We don't take cabs, they're too expensive. If you pay me for the petrol I'll come. Anyway, where will you get the money for a cab from?" I hung up.

So I auditioned for and got the coveted role on Footballers' Wives – my dream, right? Ironically, terrorists attacked London that day. They bombed all means of transport the very day I got the part, so I should have had an inkling what was about to happen...

So I'm back in England, working in an environment where I'm on the same page as the actors. I still had the dodgy American accent because it worked perfectly for the pretentious cow I created. I was living with my mother, which wasn't brilliant, but I enjoyed being around my nephews. My brother was in jail, no surprises there, and I was working fourteen-hour days and doing what I love to do in London, and the chickens had not yet come home to roost! Ah, here they come now, I can hear the flapping of their little wings.

One day I was learning lines for my biggest scene, the one after Liberty and Tremaine's wedding, where I got to work with the impeccable Joan Collins (Eva). This was the most complicated role I had ever had. One day my mother came in with the usual bailiff letter, because whenever she smells money she goes on a fix-me trip. This one was alarming: the house I was staying in had a full year of arrears on it. This meant I would be homeless unless something was done quickly; if I didn't shell out several thousand pounds for her. That's not quite the headspace you need to be in when you're filming your career shot! But I paid it and tried to look on the bright side.

At the same time, something strange was happening with my sister's kid. The authorities were trying to take him away from her because of her husband's drinking so there were police at the door and angry calls. The family unit had split, with the two sisters ganging up against me and my mother. My mother didn't say the right thing to the cops, and there were differing stories about how much I was involved, which was crazy. I was locked in my room at my mother's council house desperately holding on to my lines and my sanity.

Then my brother was paroled and I remember being relieved that I could bury my head in the Bible because without it I would have been drinking and fighting with the rest of them. At least my family could finally see my work rather than missing everything because of the different transmission schedules between the US and UK. But my mother had done it again; pulled the rug out from under me. I needed every penny I could get to get away from her and set up my own crib in London.

The Footballers' Wives set was my saving grace. Laila Rouass, who played Amber, was so welcoming; she is a very funny, special lady. She was gorgeous and classy, as you would imagine, and had a razor sharp wit, which I didn't expect. We spent the first few days of my arrival excitedly talking about Hollywood. She would ask me 'what's so and so like'? It was fun and welcoming; I needed that. Plus there were sausage rolls and cups of tea – how could I not be charmed?

I got yelled at by the director, Richard Signy (to whom I am eternally grateful to for any part he played in casting me), for yakking absentmindedly to Sarah Barrand (SB), who played Shannon, through someone else's take. I would never have done that in Hollywood, but being at home and getting carried away by the atmosphere on set I dropped my guard. I chastised myself all the way home and vowed I would never let that happen to me again. I wasn't exactly nervous but I was concerned. I needed to focus and I probably seemed quite stuck up. I wasn't, but although you'd never guess it when I have my strong woman mask on, I'm a bit socially awkward. After the first day or so, I didn't hang out with anyone but my co-star Chucky Venice. He was the one I had to look as though I loved passionately on screen and had had an enduring five-year relationship with.

I have the attention span of a gnat, so while everybody's laughing and joking, I have to stay in character or I won't know where I am and it won't match in the edit. Gillian Taylforth helped me tremendously with this. I had a scene with her (which was later cut) in which I was supposed to have been mauled by a fan. We were all cramped into this little toilet. Glamorous, huh? The producer, director and camera crew all peering at the new gal.

It was one of those stories that gives the viewer the back story. I don't really like those scenes as they are much harder for me to act. SB is from the Liverpool area, and so even though I had this transatlantic accent my first day at work, I suddenly sounded like I was the fifth Beatle! Probably thinking he had booked the wrong girl, the director very gently said: "No love, it's OK, do what you were doing in the audition." Of course in the audition I had breezed in from LA with a full-blown Californian accent.

So I was with two 'footie wives', a Cockney and a Scouser, in the toilets feeling like I was auditioning all over again. The script said that Liberty was crying but I just didn't see it that way. She was a fighter not a crier, but being the method actress I was I had held myself off from people all day, keeping myself to myself so I could do whatever I needed to do to be in the right emotional space when I was called. So I had a lot going on.

Let's recap: this was my first scene in a major TV show. There was already a difference of opinion and a wrong accent, so how could I negotiate? I try again. Anyway, I was suddenly dizzied by the fact that 'Kathy Beale' was in the scene. That's who Gillian Taylforth was to me the last time I was in the country during her long stint in Eastenders. Eight hours into my day of emotional misery – the preparation I was doing to be ready when he called me – the director told me Liberty wouldn't cry in that scene. I was relieved that he had had the same instinct as me, but I was also emotionally drained. I wished he had told me about eight hours earlier! But at least I could let all my emotions recede and be 'present' in the scene.

I think, 'right then, onto the task at hand'. I felt the anxiety of it all right in that moment. The relaxation that is key for an actor went out the window and I felt faint. Gilly, star that she is, grabbed my hand and looked directly into my eyes, steadying me somehow. I felt her saying it was going to be OK, and it was. Ben Richards (Bruno), Helen Latham (Lucy), Jesse Birdsall (Roger) and Joan Collins all took to me instantly; we had a good time together. I was always happy to see them and they were always happy to see me.

Jesse even arranged to take me to dinner with his wife and daughter because I had to work on my birthday. I tried to organise drinks and couldn't get anyone to come out with me as we had an early call the next day. It was very smart of everyone to go home, but it still felt bad. He intuitively knew I was missing California and my friends so he went out of his way for me. I'll never forget that because the kindness came just when I needed it most.

Why is it that you can't have everything? Ours is a generation of women that want it all: career, babies, hot sex, fulfilment, money in the bank, beautiful clothes and an amazing home. In California, I have the best friends a girl could ask for and the sun which, if I wasn't so devout in my faith, I would worship. But there was no consistent work. In England I had my family, whom I had made my peace with, and the best job for a long time but no real friends. We didn't spend a lot of time together as a working cast because it was like five separate shows; each one from the wife's perspective of life with her mate.

There was a considerable cooling after my initial arrival, especially when Zoë (Tanya) returned, as she did after the fourth episode. I like

Zoë a lot, she was nice to me on the surface, and she even joined Gilly and Angela Ridgeon in being the only ones that sponsored me for my marathon; and quite a generous amount too. She is a fabulous actress, and I totally admire her on screen.

I often told her that if it wasn't for her kicking butt consistently for the previous four years I wouldn't have had a job because the show would have been cancelled. I think she saw me as a bit of crackpot to be honest. But there was an unspoken dynamic that hifted when she came back, mainly in those around her; it was as if they had to pick sides.

One time I was talking to Jay (Carlos) when his cell phone rang and he asked me to excuse him. I stood quietly by not realising what was going on. I heard him say: "Zoë, why are your ringing me?" She was only about two feet away but the poor bugger didn't know he was breaking an unwritten rule about who he was allowed to hang out with. I actually found it funny, especially when he walked over to her. When I walked back she didn't realise I had cottoned on to the fact that she had warned him away from me, so she demurred and purred at me beautifully.

SB was Zoë's sidekick and was always trying to mess with me; her main obsession was my hair. She did it every time I walked into the trailer, a party or a scene. She is a beautiful blond with her own head of extensions, and was absolutely hilarious as her character. But she would be like: "Is that your hair?" Every day. I found it really odd. Then she would ask, "How old are you? How old are you?". "I'm sixty-three," I would say. "Is everybody happy now?"

I just kept my head down and got on with my work. From this point there was always an unspoken tension in the makeup trailer that I couldn't bear. I would walk on and say good morning and sometimes get ignored, or say goodbye when I left and have it fall on deaf ears. It was odd, but thanks to my upbringing I can thrive anywhere. A little adversity always brings out the gold in me.

I don't think girls admire each other enough. We spend so much time in our brokenness, afraid to compliment one another, afraid that if we notice that another girl is wonderful or has beautiful hair or has a great singing voice, that it somehow diminishes us. Poppycock. If I admire the fact that you are physically beautiful, will my own looks diminish? If I admire your singing voice does the fact that mine is yet undeveloped and I'm not a confident singer get highlighted? Okay, a big one for the coloured girls: if your hair swings beautifully to your waist, straight, glossy and with relative ease making you look like a goddess, does me not commenting and admiring it cause mine to grow? It's as though the withholding of a well-timed compliment will boost the withholder somehow. Fat chance! I read a letter to The Voice in which the female writer said I was ugly; that the whole cast of Footballers' Wives was beautiful except me! I wondered whether having taken the time to write it, she had become more beautiful as a result? Had she got herself a modelling or acting job because she had taken her precious time to condemn me? I read it with compassion, taking into account her frustration. She was probably sick of seeing me on TV or in the papers.

When you have a project publicity pops up all over the place for a while. It's difficult being a brown artist because there aren't as many, so people either hate on you or hope that you will be a perfect looking, acting and talking role model at all times. Not a chance! I am delightfully, frustratingly human. The major side-effect of my chosen profession is media attention, scrutiny and people wanting to trim the tall poppy.

But come on girls, we've got to be nice to one another. At one point I probably would have wanted Naomi's work, I might have even prayed for it and envied it, but that's not right; it's hers, gifted to her by God, and I would have fallen foul. She is tenacious and brilliant enough to sustain it although there have been many contenders for her crown. But it's hers and rightfully so. I learned early to applaud her, remembering what Milton had taught me: "What you criticise you cannot have."

Perhaps if I had been lying around in my fury criticising her, writing pointless letters to The Voice, I never would have got off the couch and on the road to my ultimate destiny, which is unfolding even now. In Milton's class we were taught to learn from the successful ones; to copy what they were doing until we found our own way, not to bludgeon them with our own fear and imaginary lack. The church has taught me that we are all part of one body and that we each have different gifts for a reason: so that everything gets done. I subscribe to that.

When Gilly was on set she killed us laughing with impressions and show tunes; what a funny and secure woman. My favourite Gilly madness was a crazy vibrato pub singer she used to do. The best times for me were when Chuck and I worked in the set house. It was just about acting and bringing out the best in each another. I often wonder if the girls thought I was Liberty, as I often take on a lot of the traits of the character I'm working on. I was under immense pressure: living in my mother's house I did nothing but rant and rave at home. I was trying to maintain peace and not have my life looted, while also trying to create a believable character.

Liberty my character was truly moody, so rather than create enemies I would be silent. Perhaps my silence was misconstrued and created enemies anyway. I'm not that great at small talk and I'm not that into current affairs or the latest boy band, so I kept myself to myself. Liberty was deeply insecure, so I had to deal with my own insecurities, which continually reared their ugly heads. I just knew I had come too far to socialise and make friends at the expense of this opportunity, this great role.

One of the producers complained to the agency and said: "She's so nice, but so desperate to fit in. She needs to just chill and she'll make friends." That was the first week. The same agent told me someone had said: "She can be a bit of a diva." That was after the second week. You can't win! I am as working class as you can get, but people who don't know me love to say that about me.

The bottom line is, if I have a character to create or a difficult scene to pin down, I won't be talking to anyone, not even Chucky who was in at least sixty percent of all my scenes and was like a brother to me. Not even the director, unless it's about the work. I can't do small talk prior to filming. I'm amazed at actors who can chit chat and then fully immerse themselves in a scene; I am not gifted with that skill yet.

I also had an odd experience with one of the assistant directors (AD) in Zoë and SB's camp. We were driven to work, a veritable luxury, but since I lived in 'sarf Landon', a situation developed between me and the AD where he would bring me in hours early. I didn't say anything as he was in the 'in crowd' and I had work to do, but it got to the point where I would bring my duvet and sleep in the car and then in the trailer until they called me. Finally, one day he brought me in and the trailers weren't even ready so I called the producer. I'd had five months of this. The producer was between a rock and a hard place: he needed me in on time, and it could always be argued that the AD was covering his derrière rather than torturing me.

That call to the producer basically signed my death warrant; the AD immediately upped the torture. They would now leave me in all kinds of strange places claiming they didn't have a car to send me back in, though curiously there were always cars for everybody else. I was left everywhere; Potters Bar was my favourite. He wouldn't allow me to drive in, and would never let me know ahead of time which days there would be a shortage of cars. Oh the joy.

At this time Chuck and I shared a trailer. Nothing ever happened in that trailer, but since we were boy and girl, I think everybody imagined we were having it away like rabbits. The truth is he's very handsome. I was delighted when I auditioned with him, and wanted him to get the part because I knew we would smash it with the chemistry. You can't act that: it's either there or it isn't.
I always played that up when I talk about him, but after a wicked whisper in The Mirror about me never meeting his girlfriend, she probably started thinking that I was dreaming about her man. I had no interest, it was purely professional. I shared a trailer with him for two

reasons: because on screen we needed to look like we were completely comfortable with each other, and because I needed an ally. Occasionally you had to share with someone, so we chose each other because it made the most sense. The AD flipped out again, he and several others hated us being in the trailer together, and boy did the tongues wag!

He ended up putting us as far from one another as he humanly could, but each lunchtime Chuck would knock on my door and we would hang out. Liberty Baker fell in love with Tremaine Gidigbi as was necessary for the script. Phina Oruche and Chucky Venice became great working partners and allies. That man is hilarious and oozes charm, but he would kill me if we got together. I had no desire to meet his girlfriend, but that doesn't mean I was after her man – I respect her. Please, girl, get a grip! I have too much self-respect and way too much to lose to be banging this man in a trailer. Plus, I was celibate. I was literally saving it for my husband-to-be, whoever that would be. I had been waiting two years! I also think I was still gun-shy after my Wild Wild West experience with Will and Jada.

I definitely understand why actors get confused and think that if they play lovers they should be lovers or that they are in love. The soul-bearing and intimacy involved in preparing such scenes is heady stuff. From my experience in Milton's class I had seen time after time, girl after girl, fall for their acting partners, and then they always did a terrible job of the acting. They were having real feelings and trying to hide the fact from the world, which made the passionate relationship they were trying to convey on screen null and void.
I was vindicated: it was well worth the gamble of flying to London to audition for Footballers' Wives.

I was trying to balance my mad, high-profile work and personal faith, and had people constantly misinterpreting me, especially if they could get a headline or two out of it! Praise God, though, all my dreams started coming true. I was in London, in my own home, and was working on two hit shows at the same time. I was getting great reviews and went on to win Favourite TV Star at the Screen Nation

Awards 2006 for Footballers' Wives. It was especially sweet for me because it was voted for by the public. I was chuffed to bits.
Scallies of the world unite! I had to pinch myself working with Joan Collins. I thought I had died and gone to actors' heaven.

Chapter Fourteen: Truly, madly, deeply

Every good thing must come to an end. Footballers' Wives was eventually cancelled which, in TV land is inevitable; there are no sure things. I was desperate in the summer of 2006: desperately lonely, annoyed, sad and a little lost in terms of what to do next. I had ballasted myself against a house that it looked like I couldn't afford to live in. I was too close to the family and couldn't seem to get through to my brother. It turned out he was back at Her Majesty's pleasure. I wasn't able to get away from the drama and the madness.

The sun worshipper in me had lost patience with the weather and I couldn't motivate my agent to work on my behalf. He had five actors from Footballers' Wives to find jobs for. The phone rang often, but people wanted me to do everything for free. It seemed like it was all for their benefit so people could photograph me or just say I would be somewhere. I was having difficulty getting through the days and at one point I was going to hop on a plane back to LA and leave the door to the house unlocked. I have always been a gypsy and settling in a place where I couldn't act wasn't an idea that pleased me.

I got another request, this time to go to Dublin. The only reason I went was that months earlier I was supposed to go to Dublin for Lorri's baby's christening. My childhood friend had married an Irishman and I had missed her wedding because of unpredictable finances, which meant I couldn't come up with the transatlantic flight to Dublin from LA at the time. Since it was just over the Irish Sea I thought the least I could do was go and wet the baby's head, but a combination of my mother letting me down on a lift to the airport and me trying to get my car into the long stay car park at the last minute left me too late for Aer Lingus. The icing on the cake for this trip was that I was able to take a mate. I chose my brother's ex-partner because she had stood by him and me through thick and thin, and because she is a right mad cow, so I knew we'd have a laugh. Boy did I need one! The trip was a blast. Irish broadcaster TV3 brought all of its soap stars from Hollyoaks, Coronation Street, Emmerdale and Footballers' Wives together.

It was my birthday while I was there, and I didn't need to create a way to mark it. I had never been to Dublin before, but man did I enjoy myself. At one point I went back to the hotel and my mate went off to hang out with Louis Walsh and Keith Duffy. She has children, so when she goes out she really goes out! I was happy for her but I can't party like that; they called me a lightweight.

The next morning there was still no sign of her when it was time to check out. She finally arrived, still drunk, and we got into the cab for the airport. In the check-in queue she told me to hide: there was an annoying paparazzo from the night before stalking around the airport. I looked dreadful. I had no makeup on and the ill-effects of the previous night's booze were emanating from every pore. I slid onto the floor; I really didn't need my face captured at this precise moment.

I started talking to two drunk English men in the queue beside me, and then all of a sudden, out of nowhere, I started talking to a gorgeous Italian man. Everybody else faded into the background. The conversation was silly. He said: "I'm Italian," which based on his looks was superfluous, and I told him "I live in London", which based on where the flight was heading was fairly obvious too. He told me he was going to the Natural History Museum in Kensington for a meeting.

Normally I am very confident with men, at least on the surface, so the tongue-tied madness I experienced at this moment was all new to me. I always picked guys that wouldn't challenge my heart too much so that I could stay focused on my career; some little boy I could leave, who wouldn't bother me with his needs or opinions, or make me change or grow in any way. I had no choice but to give in to the vulnerability. My constant prayer to God had been, when You select a man for me make sure it's so different that I can see Your mighty hand in it. I lost my mind and have never found it since.

The man was Stefano, the love of my life. It was love at first sight, I felt like a thunderbolt had hit me. I hate all those ridiculous clichés and here I was right in the middle of one. Our flight was delayed, so at one point he walked towards me and pretended to look at the display. I'm much more direct, so I asked him if he wanted to get his stuff and sit next to me. He did and I showed him the morning's papers in which I had appeared. I have no idea why I showed them to him, but I guess it was because I was all tongue-tied and coy.

When our flight finally boarded I ran into the priority queue. Stefano wasn't as nimble as me and got lost in the shuffle, so I put my hand out, grabbed him by the wrist and declared: "The sexy nerd comes with me". He blushed like a Japanese school girl, which, on a man as gorgeous as him, was hot! He's a marine biologist and is so refreshing because he hasn't a clue how beautiful he is. He has an Italian accent, so everything he says is sexy. He is also brilliant, speaking three languages fluently and able to get by in a few others. I was in like Flynn!

On the flight, emboldened by having my sister-in-law there, I invited him to my birthday dinner. He told me right way: "I can't make it, I have to be back in Dublin for a friend's christening." I gave him my number in case he changed his mind. We talked about absolutely everything. My sis, sensing something was going down, pretended to be asleep. We actually took a photo of us together that very moment, and on reflection you can see we were already goners!

He showed me a film of his thirteen-month-old nephew sitting on his lap. If I wasn't already gone I would have been by then, because he was so tender with him. He asked me if I wanted to have kids and I said that it was too late for me.

I had a meeting to get to when the plane landed. I was going to meet the producers of I'm A Celebrity Get Me out Of Here to sell my soul to the devil. To this day he teases me because as soon as the plane hit the ground I rang him to say "it was very nice to meet you", all cold and disconnected. In hindsight I think it was a defence mechanism; I had no idea how to choose a decent bloke, and had often joked that my 'chooser' was broken. I had been celibate for two-and-a-half years so I was about to step off the plane and put him out of my mind. Men are usually a distraction and aren't worth the both; that was my default setting.

The next morning I was in church and he called me. I told him I was in a meeting, which was technically true, but I was a bit embarrassed to explain why I was at a prayer meeting at 8am on a Saturday morning. That is my secret rocket fuel, but to people who don't live that way you sound nuts, especially as the media portrays the far right of Christianity more than anything else.

But he said: "Bizarrely enough, I'm going to come to your party tonight, but don't marginalise me, please don't stick me in a corner." He called me later in the day and told me he had bought a new shirt especially and asked me what I would be wearing. I was trying to be cool because my sister-in-law and mates were there getting ready to go out with me. We were all girly and mad, it was a very funny time. He sent me a text asking me where I was as he was already in the restaurant "patiently waiting". I fibbed and said we were five minutes away, which was silly since we still had to pick up a neighbour on the way.

I finally got to the restaurant. He was alone as he was the first one there and he had a beautiful bunch of flowers. He sat next to me all night and whispered to me in Italian: "Sei la donna più bella del mondo" (you are the most beautiful girl in the world). How could I resist that? He danced with me when we headed over to the dance floor and when we left I asked my friend to drop him in Brixton, but he kept trying to kiss me in the car and begged me to let him come to my house since he was leaving the next day. I had two girls staying there so there was no chance; I wasn't going to act like a slapper with them in tow! We dropped him off, much to his chagrin.

When I got home we started texting up a storm. I'd had a glass of cheap rosé wine and, mixed with the champers, it really hit me. The next thing I remember was one of my mates telling me he was on the doorstep. Apparently, as the alcohol took effect, I had got bolder and invited him over. He arrived with his suitcase in tow and we never looked back.

I journeyed through life unable to be close to anyone until I met my sweet, beautiful boyfriend in 2006. I was able to tell him everything written here, it would have been impossible to have an intimate relationship with him otherwise. He is quite attuned to my feelings anyway, so if I didn't tell him what was going on he would always inquire about the fluctuations in my emotions. What a caring man. Six weeks later he asked me to marry him and a year after that we actually tied the knot! What can I say, miracles happen and love at first sight exists. He told me: "You are in credit. You have had a deficit of care, but I will care for you." Bellisimo!

Chapter Fifteen: My God shall supply

I took part in a 'reality' show. Note that I'm using the word 'reality' really, really loosely. I was all too easily wooed from my stance that I would never take part in one, having deemed reality shows beneath my calling. The stark reality was I was flat broke and needed the money! I should have known something wasn't right, though. Firstly, my agent Pierre didn't get me the job, another agent who was chasing me at the time offered it to me. They were setting up all kinds of meeting for me to meet TV executives to discuss the possibility of presenting. I didn't fancy it, but I didn't have much choice.

This agent gamely sent me in to see the producers of I'm a Celebrity. I had no idea what the show was. I vaguely remember seeing something about it while I was in my Footballers' Wives trailer, but since I had never seen it and had only been back in the country five months I didn't know what it was. After sitting in the meeting for a little while, a few things became apparent. They had been calling Pierre for a few weeks, perhaps even months, and he had turned it down without mentioning it to me. And, since I clearly wasn't there to become a presenter, thank goodness I sat and listened before spouting out my views on presenting the show. Ant and Dec who? I had been to one of their Saturday night shows, but I didn't know who they were; I can be so dumb at times. Things were all a bit pear-shaped. Yes, I'd had a wondrous return to Britain, originally getting a three-year contract (which are about rare as a three-titted dog) and immediately did what any actor with a long contract would do. I ran out and eagerly bought a house. And not just any old house: a luxury, fully restored 1850s cottage.

I was possibly swayed by the splendour I worked among on a daily basis on Footballers' Wives. It's risky because it's television, a land of shifting focus and finances. One day you're hot and the next you're not, but as a true believer in Christ I felt God would supply all my needs according to his riches in glory.
I finished the first year of my contract feeling proud and settled. My career was going well and I had my autonomy back, but then ITV

decided not to make any more of the programme, which stunned us all. It possibly gutted me more than most because I was out on a limb financially; every penny I had earned was spent. And trust me, I'd had a very good salary.

I was too old to live with my mother and I knew I could never lay myself open to her, that I had to maintain my autonomy. I was tired of having nothing but newspapers and magazines to show for my efforts. As nice as that can be for the ego, it's pretty useless unless you calculate it as kindling to start a fire when your ass is out in the cold, as it often is in this godforsaken business. Don't get me wrong, I love what I do and I love the nomadic lifestyle that comes with it. But when you get to a certain point in life, a certain level of business acumen and notoriety you get tired of not having the things you feel you should have: like decent housing. The cancellation announcement left me reeling.

In California I would have known precisely what to do. I would have had a full market of acting work to be auditioning for as I knew the seasons when you can get cast for pilots and when you can get cast for films. I was well versed with lean times and would have gone straight back to selling cosmetics for Mary Kay, a support job I had loved and heavily relied on in the past. But in London I felt paralysed. I didn't have my contacts here and didn't know the British way of doing things. I was also very high profile, so that adds extra pressure. You can hardly go down the chippy looking for a job, though I would have if I could have!

My agent seemed to be constantly asleep or on holiday. I would call to ask about things I'd come across and he would tell me about his boyfriend's ill health or his latest trip, or he'd actually be on a trip. I asked him what was I supposed to do with my time and he quipped: "Start drinking, become an alcoholic, go to rehab". Very funny, except I was in real trouble… So the relationship with my agent was cooling.

I did a quick stint on The Bill after writing a letter to the casting people. Then I did a quick impersonation of Lauryn Hill for Celebrity Stars in their Eyes. Think about it, a non-singer singing for her supper on National TV; I must have been desperate to even go down that route! Don't hold your breath, no recording contracts were offered and I advised myself to stick to the day job!

But I never quite managed to get myself a job. In wild frustration I went to the dole office. I had vowed never to darken its doors after the last time, when I was a teenager living in squalor off the Old Kent Road. In hindsight, my experience there was funny, but at the time it was humiliating and frustrating. I decided to go in there looking terrible, wearing a hat and baggy clothing as I was often recognised and my ego couldn't take being spotted in there. I went in and signed a form while a very laconic woman filed her nails and eyed me. I asked her a question and she basically told me to "shut up and wait". She then proceeded to tell me she was "at lunch".

Then a procession of gangster rapper types came in and she demurred. She swiftly came off her lunch break to help them. Encouraged by how nice she was to them, I tried again. Again she growled that she was "out to lunch". You would think that I would have learned a lesson or two, that I'd have had some common sense, but no! I allowed her to get at me again because I was foolish enough to stay. I wondered miserably what the £56 would do for me and my expenses anyway, seeing as they had probably run into the thousands by this point.

One of her colleagues came in and seemed nicer, so I tried her. Luckily she called me over and sat me down. Since the desks are only suitable for five-year-olds I was practically on the nasty woman's desk anyway. I tried to grasp for my dignity, but it was long gone. I started whispering the answers to what seemed like a lot of questions for £56.

Suddenly, the first woman recognised me. "Er, ain't you that girl from Footballers' Wives?" "Erm, no," I hissed, horrified. "Yes you are," she insisted, thrilled at having me as her prey. No one loves a 'celeb' on the ropes as much as the British! She kept on doggedly, enlisting her colleague for help. "Don't she look like that girl from the telly?" she asked her. Her colleague, a brilliant woman, looked at me for what felt like two hours and then weighed it up and said, with authority: "No, this girl hasn't got a pot to piss in. I'm not being funny, but the girl from the show is gorgeous and stylish; she wouldn't be seen dead in here." After I had picked up my chin and my ego from the floor I started thinking about how to escape without raising suspicion. She added: "No, you're probably right, but I heard that girl signs on here and that she ran that marathon. And she got twenty grand an episode for Footballers' Wives. I actually felt physically sick, but I played the game, got through my appointment and once again vowed never to set foot in the dole office again, even though I was unemployed and, as my mother never stops telling me, the dole is my entitlement. On the planet my sweet but roguish mother inhabits, everything is your entitlement.

Right after that I had a letter from the Council Tax office claiming I owed them all kinds of dough. But with my last pay check I had made a block payment, so I was baffled by this. I wondered how I could possibly owe the feckers anything and I was so strapped for cash I just ignored them. But then I started receiving notes from the bailiffs that for once weren't generated by my mother and certainly weren't love notes. Finally, the day of reckoning arrived so I went in to see them. My years of living in an American society where the actor is cherished blinded me to reality.

Foolishly thinking I was going into the type of help session American agencies hand out to actors like cough drops I, much to my bemusement, found myself in a hearing with two very serious claim assessors. They were holding up my unemployment claim on which I hadn't declared any of my income post-Footballers' Wives. In my haste I hadn't filled the form in properly because I had no intention of signing on or receiving the money! However it was Exhibit A in the case of the Council versus Phina Oruche. Stunned, I laughed my head off, as I often do in bizarre situations. But it was no laughing matter to them. Eventually I left the hearing, went outside and asked a lovely middle-aged woman what on earth was going on. With the click of a mouse she realised that since I lived alone, 25% could be cancelled and the money I had paid the year before killed off most of the remaining debt. It was sheer madness. Why I wasn't able to achieve that with the copious amount of paperwork I had filled out and the many phone calls I had made is only the good Lord's guess.

My DFS sofa, which I had bought on hire purchase, was threatening to get up and leave because I had structured the payments to start when I went back to work, but I never did get back to work. Added to this, my lovely friend James had lent me half the deposit on my house so I could move in that year and not the next; to give me some self-respect and prevent me from having to live with my mother, God bless him. Even though he had never mentioned it, I knew he had taken it out of his mortgage reserve. So if my ship was sinking, which it was, I desperately didn't want to take him with me. Pressure!

In short, I needed a job. And fast. So I'm a Celebrity Get Me Out of Here it was. They had come after me early in the summer but I wasn't interested. Even though I needed a job, I didn't think I would do well with the starvation thing, the 24/7 camera thing and the sharing my life with eleven strangers thing. How right I was.

The whole notion of celebrity is strange; I always thought it was being celebrated for your work, your craft. I think the whole notion of doing I'm a Celebrity made me both fearful about opening my life to a fickle press and laugh my head off, if I'm honest. Who in their right mind wants to be examined round the clock and have their behaviour edited the way they care to show you; allowing them to create a story about you when you are hungry, freaked out and weak?

I love the craft of acting, using my life history and emotions to express what has been written. That's what I'm good at and trained to do. The downside of my job is that you lose your privacy. I left myself wide open by participating in the show and blame myself for it totally. I decided to do it for my own personal financial gain: to save my house and to pay back my friend. I also thought it would be a great opportunity to help a young boy named Keiton Knight, who needed half a million pounds for a lifesaving operation. Apparently you make a fantastic amount for charity by participating.

With those things in mind, I sacrificed my privacy and decided to go into the jungle. Immediately I had the hangers-on calling and texting me. Fortunately, as I was sworn to secrecy, that only happened the day before my departure because The Daily Star had announced the "Z-list celebs" who were taking part. I was excited to be on the Z-list; at least I was on a list! I was ranked as an outsider and my odds of winning were a hundred to one. Well that depends on your perspective. I had won already: in one fell swoop I had got out of bone-crushing debt, so whatever happened after that was gravy for me. But enter the celebrity circus and all those who jumped on the bandwagon.

All kinds of people started to step forward with their agendas. A couple who ran a charity started bombarding me with strange requests about what I should do with the money and asked me if I could support lots of kids and not just Keiton. I was upset by it. Like Madonna and her Malawian baby, I was trying to help, and I would rather help one fully than many badly, or none at all. Then a sleazy newspaperman who I had made "friends" with earlier in the year and had covered me favourably from Footballers' Wives to The Bill started texting me, asking do an exit interview with me when I left. He pleaded with me not to say anything to the man from the same paper who was in Australia covering the event.

I was staying in my mother's house during the time leading up to the show, and a young, cheeky journalist from The Daily Mail blagged her way into my mother's front room and started to question her. Crikey! I only realised she was there because I heard the doorbell ring and had come downstairs to offer my mother's guest a coffee. I was downstairs in the kitchen putting the kettle on when my mother asked me how long it had taken me to run the marathon. I wondered why she would want to know that, so I pushed open the living room door to see an eager young woman with a pad and pen questioning my naive mother. The journo paled and looked panic-stricken when she saw me.

I was like "who are you?" and when she told me she was from The Daily Mail I lost my temper a bit and told her to get out. I walked her to the door, softening a bit, as her ambition mirrored mine at her age, and said: "I'm not being rude, but this is not the way to do it. If you want to interview us then you make an appointment, you don't blag your way in." She told me I was being rude, and I was shocked and unprepared at the lows to which a tabloid journalist will go to get some fodder for a story. The next day another eager young girl with a pad and paper was on the doorstep, but my mother had been briefed this time and she didn't get in. I realised they send the young girls around as a ploy to someone my mother's age as they probably look as though they could have been an old school friend of mine. Clever stuff!

I was photographed at the airports, both checking in and landing. When I got to Australia they asked me to take off my shades. Honey, I had been in those clothes for twenty-six hours and counting, plus my suitcase never arrived so I looked like hell in high heels. So, no, darling, there was no chance of those shades coming off!

I was in the jungle as soon as I got there... a media jungle. Even though there were days to go before the beginning of the show, I was on lockdown immediately so I wouldn't bump into the other contestants. I had a 24/7 bodyguard so I couldn't go anywhere or do anything without asking permission. I had no clothes but I was bought a couple of swimsuits by production, thank God.

I was photographed working out and doing my daily run on the beach in my swimsuit the day before going to meet the others and was interviewed by the lovely and very stylish Kelly Osbourne for her ITV2 commentary show. Then I was interviewed for something else – I didn't quite know what – and then I was on the phone with The Star, The Sun and someone else. I was asked if I fancied anyone and if, since I had lost my suitcase, I would be wearing any knickers in the jungle! I cheekily said no, because I didn't have any. They span that into a headline story! Whatever I had signed myself up for it was way beyond my comprehension.

My strategy was this... I had none. I would be myself, warts and all. One of my sisters said I should have gone in there and put on an act, created a character. But that's already done for you by production; they assign everybody an archetypal character and cut the footage around that. I was the bitch, based on my Footballers' Wives profile and based on the way strong black women are portrayed in our media. I played along at first when we were doing the sound bites and stuff in London. I suppose I could have put on a sweet as pie act, but I'm not as sweet as pie.

And boy did I feel set up to be the bad, tough black girl from the start! I knew the hunger, the lack of privacy, the strategies, the egos and the inane conversation would do me in, and I was right. I am real, I can tell you. I really didn't care about winning; I just didn't want to be voted off first. I have the following regrets about the jungle. Everyone else hired publicists to protect them while they were in there and to control what could be said in the press. I was naive enough not to as I didn't realise how popular the show was. I didn't do my homework or understand it and I certainly didn't see that I was handing them exactly what they needed; that they would be able to edit the footage to make me look like the stereotypical, fierce angry black girl. What a load of cobblers!

I came along with my Bible and my Scouse-American demeanour and they didn't know what to make of me. I took my Bible as my luxury item, not to preach, not to grab attention, but because I read it daily: to lift me up when I'm down, to comfort me when I'm confused, to inspire me, and to give me comprehension and guidance to work through tough situations. It's the manual, man! I find the answers to all my dilemmas in there, so I needed it.

Now it's been said that I'm a bad example of Christianity. I beg to differ: a Christian is someone who knows they (and everybody else) need help from God, and that's me. It's someone who wants to get under His anointing; someone who has decided to try and live by the manual that was written by the creator. This is very difficult under normal circumstances, but to do it half starved under the glare of the media is not pretty. I can tell you that without God I could never have made it through most of my life, but especially not this part.

I noticed during the very first group meeting and photo call that there was a preference for those who later became the final three; it was always a three-horse race. As a group we got on famously, so much so that I was shocked by the final edit. Sophie Anderton had told me they had edited her to look bad on Love Island, but I didn't understand what she meant until I left the jungle, read the papers and saw the footage. What was chronicled did not reflect my experience at all.

I am brutally honest because I come from a place where fraud ruled; that's safety for me. I am also a nutter, funny and a bit of a blagger. Gone were my jokes, my humour and my caring side. The times I had read Scripture to David and Faith when they were having a hard time were gone too. Now come on, I know reading the Bible doesn't make for compelling viewing, but there seemed a definite slant to only show the tough side of me. I want to know why, out of all the Spice girls, it's the black one that was called Scary Spice. All the others had cutesy monikers. It seems we can be portrayed as sporty and strong but not soft, vulnerable or alluring.

Look at Naomi, she is demonised. Admittedly, she hands the press a lot of ammunition and doesn't help herself, but I know firsthand of so many others who have their bad behaviour hidden for years and then it comes out eventually, no matter how well protected a star is. Like her supermodel friend who was finally exposed for snorting cocaine after years of being shielded by the people who made money from her. After a minor slap on the wrist she earned more, would potentially go on to reoffend, and was held up as some kind of national hero. Is it because she is white? I sincerely hope not but, conspiracy theories aside, it makes me wonder.

Every time I had a disagreement with Jan or Scott about beds or beans or anything silly they would show me standing up for myself. They never showed what was said before or why I was adamant about not trading beds. The thing was we were all supposed to rotate beds so that everyone had a moment in the tree house, but after two or three people switched no one else would. So on Malandra's first day, when they added hammocks to the camp and suggested another rotation, I maintained that I wouldn't do it unless everybody else did it. I offered up my bed to sleep in the hammock permanently, but they never put that in the edit. The result was I looked petty, territorial and bizarre.

There was some cobblers about me eating too much and stealing food, but there wasn't a chance of that – there never was any extra food! I lost a stone in there. I did (and do) eat rapidly, so I looked like a glutton. But having been the youngest child, it was smart to eat that way or you lost the best bits of food. There was much made of the fact that when I was camp leader I asked to be called "queen" for the day, which was a piss-take based on the Scouse use of the word. That makes me laugh. There was also much made about the fact that I have a blended accent. This is because I lived in the US for more than a decade and had to learn American dialects for the many parts I crafted over there. I couldn't be bothered to put on a voice that isn't true to my life experience. So I read somewhere that I am a pretend American, how funny!

Certain members of the group were exempt from trials and chests that were physically difficult. That was just wrong. Why were they there if they weren't fit enough to participate? Then when I swam with crocodiles and won immunity and a meal each for the girls, the rules were switched. But by then I knew the show better; it was all part of the game. We were blended back in with the lads so we only got half a meal each.

Even though they provided me with DVDs of the show before I went in, I was unable to watch them because I was afraid if I saw the show I wouldn't want to take part, which was true. I remember people talking about the jungle on-set the year before and I thought at the time it looked like a load of old nonsense. But because I was uninitiated I was annoyed after the debacle with the chest where I playfully bit Scott, who I'd considered a friendly face on the show (even after he banged on about it to cover his inadequacies for doing badly in every chest and trial, and has subsequently tried to sell the story to every paper that would listen).

After that I was thrown back into the lion's den, and wasn't sure what kind of welcome I would get. The boys were wonderful to my face about it, especially Matt Willis, who was there on the day of the chest trial and handled the bizarre events with subtle class. I often told him he was well brought up and very grounded; he still has all his schoolmates even though he's had such wonderful success with the band. In hindsight, I'm not surprised that he was so popular. What a gent. I'm so glad he won! It was a lesson to all of us: he quietly just got on with everything and everyone.

From day one they had splashed me all over the papers in swimsuits looking sexy, which wasn't all bad, to be honest. But they initially thought me and Myleene might duke it out to see who was the 'camp babe', playing up the age-old idea that girls can't get on. What they didn't know was that she and I had met at the National Television Awards the year before and had kept in touch.

She is classy, strong, very hardworking and has a brilliant business mind. I love Myleene, so there was no contest. Plus I'm older than her, and have done a lot of the things I know she aspired to do; I know she wanted to break into modelling, for example. I wasn't at all interested in that title, so they changed their focus, constantly showing Myleene in a wet bikini and in the shower. Ironically, Myleene was quite shy about her lovely figure while I, being a tomboy and quite athletic, am not. It was odd that I was never shown showering; was the inference that I didn't wash?

What message are they sending here? I swam every day so I was constantly wet and in my swimsuit, but they were no longer interested in me being the camp babe. I think it was just decided I was the camp baddie or the stirrer. I often speak my mind if someone or something is bothering me. I would ask someone outside the situation about it, then go and talk to the person; the training for this came from my relationship with my sisters. I could then usually then go to the person without anger.

One of the remnants from childhood is that I'm impatient and have an excitable, hot temper. Add the blunt way I state my case, and I basically handed the editors a way (especially if they took away the resolution of the issue) for me to look like I talked about everyone behind their backs as they generally showed the confrontation and not the make-up afterwards. I have since learned to go directly to the source.

For the record, I admire Jan Leeming. She's older than my mother and did six awesome trials. She did things I wouldn't do, especially eating the animal testicles. There's no way on planet earth I would have participated in that, so as that's the final trial there is no way I could never have won. Can you imagine the hacks' glee seeing a black girl eating the unspeakable part of an animal like a savage? I didn't need to hand them any more ammunition.

Jan and I had an initial clash of personality but because we worked it out I feel that I probably could be friendly with her now. Friendship that hasn't been through trial is usually a fair-weather one, which isn't worth anything. At least with Jan I know now what I would get. I had no idea she had been married and divorced five times! When I learned that I felt immeasurable compassion for her; it must be hard being in your sixties and not having anyone in your corner.

Having no lifetime partner, that's tough for a woman of any age! Or having to downsize several times, and feeling you didn't get the appropriate financial reward for the hard work you had done. I could relate to that. Although I was four months into the affair of a lifetime with Stefano and was finally being loved in a passionate, cherishing, nurturing way, I had previously been the career woman with no love in her life. It's hard even in your late thirties when you're not sure whether you've been left on the shelf.

But come on people, get real. Why the heck were we sitting in the Australian jungle if we had it all together? There probably wasn't one among us that didn't need to be there financially, no matter what the papers 'guestimated' about our incomes. Others were also trying to restart or reshape their careers.

Whatever our reasons, the British bash anyone who dares to raise their head above the parapet. I went in with the American idea that the celebrity is revered, oops! I was deemed madly competitive. Guilty as charged – I am – but only with myself. I want to do the best I can with whatever is put in front of me. I'm committed to winning; to living life to the full, whether I ruffle anyone's feathers or not.

I am responsible to God for being a good steward of my time and talents. The time between my modelling success and acting success was littered with failure. I was trying not to get too big for my britches, but my britches had become a bit too small! I was waiting for approval from the other celebs, which wasn't forthcoming, and I finally decided to do what I needed to do in order to enjoy the good days and walk out on the bad. I was constantly mocking myself with my "Rambina" comments and cries of "Womanville".

The fact of the matter is, how can you take this show seriously? It's a game! Fortunately, the intelligent public were fabulous, funny and very supportive. Fiona Phillips was my heroine; she apparently defended me on TV so that was an unexpected blessing. I had the good fortune of meeting her shortly afterwards and was able to thank her in person. She even introduced me to Matthew Wright, which led to my frequent guest panelling on The Wright Stuff, his current affairs show. Thank God for Matthew, he really has been a godsend, and for TV3 in Dublin's TVAM, their equivalent to the UK's GMTV.

Something really unexpected happened to me in Australia. There's a doctor who psychoanalyses you on the way in to make sure you're fit for the show, and then again on the way out. She was a wonderful lady of colour, so I felt really comfortable with her. I didn't really want to go to her on the way out because by the time it was over I just wanted to retreat. I felt so vulnerable, but I went to her to appease the production team.

She had this to say: "You exhibit classic signs of someone who has been traumatised repeatedly and recently." I was shocked and thought she was mad, but after a year or so it impacted me. I started to remember huge chunks of my childhood that I had subsequently forgotten or distanced myself from.

On leaving the lion's den. My thought was "Oh well, if it doesn't kill you, it will make you stronger. And at least I found my voice".

After leaving the jungle I went to see Joan Collins in An Evening with Joan Collins, her one-woman show, which her husband Percy Gibson directed. I was struck by so many things. The fact that she was still working really hard and not waiting for the phone to ring resonated with me. She had already lined up Legends, a play with Dynasty co-star Linda Evans that toured the States for 18 months. I left her presence absolutely inspired. The fact was I really didn't know what went before Dynasty; the legacy she created. I saw her with Bing Crosby, Gene Kelly and Sammy Davis Junior. She had worked alongside the legends of Hollywood from Bette Davis down.

It's amazing how, when we don't know where a person has come from, all we think about is the big success and not all the other elements that contributed to it. I relate to people thinking that actors actually are the character that gives them their break. For a while in LA it was "aren't you the girl from Buffy the Vampire Slayer?". It's the same thing here with Footballers' Wives. But wonderful as both work opportunities were, I've had a much longer career than that; I'm more than just the sum of my parts.

I got all this mock concern from people that Footballers' Wives was over, but the fact of the matter is, it was over as soon as I started it.

By this I mean that, although delighted to create such a complex character, my nature is such, and the industry is such, that you must constantly look forward. That's the way my engine works. It's almost as though once you get the film or TV show and you're shooting it, your vision must extend to what lies beyond.

I had formulated a plan with my agent before doing the reality show. We decided together that if necessary I would go back to Los Angeles for a while if the coverage from I'm a Celebrity wasn't favourable. I felt it wasn't, although at the time he said I had handled it "with class". When you leave the jungle, they drive you away in a limousine and call back to England to talk to your agent. Although there's a time difference, the producer of the show was horrified because we called Pierre several times and it went straight to answer phone on live TV.

I didn't see anything wrong with this, as I had no experience of the show and thus no expectation. But hindsight gives you 2020 vision. I should have known then what I know now: that Pierre was ashamed of the whole thing and wanted to distance himself from it. Interestingly, he didn't distance himself from the hefty fee and the commission that he truly didn't earn. He'd created one audition for me in a year! He is amazing at collecting a stable of impressive stars, but often for one reason or another you fall off the agent's hot list. I was too LA in my business thinking; I knew it in my spirit, but was too scared to confront it. So off I went, back to my comfort zone: back to the sunshine, my friends, and to Los Angeles pilot season.

I had two offers in London and another to do a free, one-night-only play in Liverpool. There were no expenses on offer and no place to stay, but I'm sure they assumed I could stay with family. Obviously, that wasn't a possibility for me, so I decided to reinvent myself in LA. I needed a new agent out there because when I left I no longer had one. I was full of confidence because I finally had a great series under my belt.

James came up with the money to place a Variety advert congratulating me on my win of a Screen Nation award. It was to be put in the LA version so that local agents could see it. This would give me a stronger footing while I was making the rounds because no one wants to take anyone on as a client in pilot season. There are too many actors on their books already, so unless they smell success or money they don't bother. They are just too busy.

It was very sweet of him, although he probably partly wanted to keep me in LA. I was suffering because I had been on the mountain top and was falling fast. The ad got put in the London and the LA version, and was in every gift bag at the BAFTAs. Oh, brother! I got a meeting with an agent immediately and they took me on, sent me to an audition for a TV show called The Unit and booked it. I tried to call London to get advice but I couldn't with my ridiculously cheap, pay-as-you-go mobile. I was in a quandary.

I called the US agent to ask them to get Pierre to call me as it was urgent and I needed his help. I was making a very generous salary shooting this drama on US TV, but I had promised to go onstage in Liverpool for free. Could they get me out of it? To this day he has never returned the call; what he did do is fire me by email. He has seen the London advert and I can see now why it made him very nervous. I can imagine all the flack he got from other actors wondering why they didn't get the same treatment. It was all really embarrassing, but it put an end to the situation of him not wanting to deal with me.

The lesson here was that if I had stayed clinging to a situation that clearly wasn't working I would have missed out on the lovely agent I have now: the delectable and deliciously glamorous Emma Engers at International Artistes. Emma has been with me through thick and thin: literally through wedding (thin), pregnancy (extremely thick) and beyond. I wish I had followed my instincts earlier but I had always wanted to stay loyal to Pierre because I credited him with getting me the audition for Footballers' Wives, which was a no-brainer when I think about it.

In the end he hid away, so we never got to resolve our issues. This was really a blessing in disguise as it gave me a chance to look at my own behaviour throughout our working relationship. I still wanted to speak to him for a long time, to fix it somehow and change the outcome. Every now and then it pops up and annoys me, but it's just my bruised ego wanting to control things; to have him not think badly of me. I've had to just grow up and move on.

Chapter Sixteen: Wedding belles

All my family drama came to a head around the time of my wedding. Don't they say a wedding brings out the best and the worst in people? From the moment I announced I was getting married, the family went into full-scale, meltdown and overdrive. If it had been a movie I would have paid to see it or longed to act out a part in it! But when it's your own life and family it's not half as entertaining. I wanted a beautiful white wedding, and to be fair that's what I got in the end. It will always be remembered as the best day of my life: the day I became a Mariani! But the drama beforehand was like a three-act play.

Oh, where to begin? My brother got recalled to jail again. He had had a brush with the law earlier in the year, and since he had been paroled less than a year before, the Home Office recalled him. Haven't they got anything better to do? He's pretty harmless, but they still revoked his prison license. I wanted him to be my best man because I love him. He is brilliant, but – like all of us – he's a victim of our upbringing. He's often seen as rogue, but he's a lovable one. The sun rises and sets in the man's heart as far as I'm concerned. You have to walk a mile in his shoes before you can judge. Of course I see all his flaws, but I still adore him. He's like a wounded soldier from the same battalion as me. Funnily enough, when I asked him to do the honours he said "we'll see". I wondered at the time what he had on that was more important than walking his baby sister down the aisle in the absence of our father. But I realise now that he knew the likelihood of him still being out of jail was slim to none. There is always more to a family story than meets the eye.

His ex-girlfriend had always been like a sister to me. She's a funny, generous, strong and crazy woman. She could do a one-woman show and leave most professional comedians in the dust. But she also has a heart of gold and supported me all year long, coming to my events and cheering me on at work.

But all of a sudden she was offended! She just dropped me cold and wouldn't answer my calls or texts. It was very worrying and I felt lost without her. It was all because I had sent an invitation with her and the kids' names on and then "only" after the names. I did this because Scousers are a cheeky lot and I didn't want a massive crowd of hangers-on at my wedding. I didn't want the phone calls asking me if 'our such and such' could come, so I decided to nip it in the bud. I didn't really see it as offensive when I wrote it but, whipped up by my sisters, she went on a drama crusade with them.

One sister had run off to the States to prevent her divorce from the alcoholic husband. I have no idea why, but that was what she decided to do. So crazy was the notion that she had the foresight to leave her child with us for safety, so she hadn't completely lost her mind, but still… I was really worried about her because she is only strong when she has no contact with him whatsoever. We prayed on the phone every day until she saw him, and then she stopped calling me and shacked up with him again!

Ah, the madness. If you knew their history you would either howl with laughter or get her committed. Love is amazing. In some ways I actually admire her capacity to love, because she has been through thick and thin with this guy. But her daughter started to miss her and act up and we all started to get edgy taking turns as carer. Then all of a sudden she came home, mad at the world. I understand that when you are in the middle of a divorce you might not feel like celebrating your younger sister's white wedding. But boy did she make it tough.

I then had four attempted robberies on my home in a period of two weeks, but luckily the criminals were inept. The first time there was a ladder left leaning against the wall that led onto my roof. It looks like it has lead on it, so the junkies were trying to rip it off. Unfortunately for them I live by a traffic light on a busy main road, so I can only imagine a double-decker bus went past and scared them off. It's not actually lead, so they would have been very disappointed having risked everything to get it off. We were blissful in bed, probably dreaming of our wedding, and didn't have a clue.

The second time I was lying in bed alone. Stefano was working away, and I woke up because I heard voices close to my head. I woke up face to face with a fat scally, who bolted on sight. His skinny mate, the lookout kid, was sitting on the fence and I had to bang on the window before he realised his mate had deserted him. He was only about fifteen years old, God bless him. They also left a really nice ladder behind.

The third time was about a week later. Stefano was home this time, and we both woke up at exactly the same moment and ran like the clappers down the hall. Stefano was starkers, screaming something unintelligible in Italian. Our window had been jimmied open and there was my laptop and purse untouched on the kitchen counter, praise God. Stefano ran after the boy and the cheeky sod was like: "Shut up man!" Like we had overreacted to our house being burgled!

The fourth and final time happened a week later. I was exhausted, so I sent a text to one of my sisters asking her to come over and spend the night with me while my nearly husband was away. She never returned it. By this time my brother's dog was installed in the yard (more about that later) and she suddenly started barking nonstop. I wasn't asleep anyway, I had stopped sleeping after the second break-in attempt because I felt like I was being targeted. There was a four-man team trying to get into the property.

Myleene went into hospital and had her baby three weeks earlier than she had anticipated, and God bless her she still called me and asked if there was anything she could do to help me get ready for my big day. She said she wasn't doing anything "but sitting in her stitches". What a gal! I declined because I didn't really want to mix my professional life with my fast-unravelling personal one.

I decided then against the whole celeb wedding shebang. I knew Myleene, Sinitta, Miss Jocelyn, Chucky Venice and my friends from Footie Wives and The Bill would have come along to wish me the best. I knew I could have sold the rights to some magazine and had photographers and the press trampling all over my wedding, denying my mates the right to take their own pictures and confiscating phones left and right. But given all the secrets and lies, I deemed it not only a terrifying thought, but a deeply inappropriate one. I didn't want anyone to get hurt so I backed away from the spotlight.

Annie hired a 1939 Royale Windsor with a chauffeur so I could arrive in style. She had asked for the family to contribute to my day and they had all said no, so she went ahead on her own and did it. She has a heart the size of Texas, that girl.

Sister number two was complaining that I was selfish because I had stopped taking her overcritical calls about who I should have as bridesmaids, telling me that my "brother would let me down or look like dung and make a show of the whole family". She said I had chosen my bridesmaids because they were thin, which was ridiculous. I had actually asked her to be my maid of honour first and my other sister and sisters-in-law if they would be bridesmaids, but they turned me down saying they didn't want to be photographed with me. Lovely!

I chose my best friend's kids Shakila and Asanti, aged ten and eleven, and had a whale of a time dressing them and being girly, which is what is supposed to happen. Sister two cried poverty. She couldn't afford a dress, or to get her hair done, get transport or book a hotel, even though our family home is in Liverpool so there were plenty of places she could have stayed. I bought her a dress under duress but she refused to try it on. Then when I asked for it back because I wanted to return it, it caused murder.

But I did need help, and fast. I didn't want to become bridezilla. Thank God that help came from my church family. They offered to help me with colour schemes and flowers and my church brother Franklyn, who had buried his mother two days earlier, came to sing and play guitar for us. Stef and I went to the funeral on the way to our wedding, with the car piled high with stuff. We had to strategically park it outside the church and take turns watching it. My church sister

Vera, along with my pastor and his wife and many of the congregation, travelled from London to Liverpool, where I eventually had my big day. I ran into DJ Ivan Freeman, who played the soundtrack to my teenage years, running off the bridezilla stress with Stefano. He gladly signed on to play our music.

I got married on my birthday – August 31, 2007 – in a manor house in Sefton Park. It was a year to the day of our first meeting. I call him my birthday gift, and he is the gift that truly keeps on giving. The weather was perfect and my brother did me proud on the day; he looked gorgeous. I have lovely pictures of him almost modelling as he signed the wedding register. It was good for him to be suited and booted, he needs reminding how glorious he can be. Sometimes when you get knocked down you can forget who you are and start looking at yourself the way society sees you. I still believe that if anyone can pull themselves back to full strength, he can.

I had wanted to get married in Rome, where my beloved is from, and where you can rely more on the weather, but I knew there was no way on God's earth we would get my family on planes and into hotels at their own expense, especially with the sisters crying about any money they had to spend, and one of them climbing over the wall of my property to ask me who was paying for their hotel rooms. I wondered what planet she was on.

And we had also decided we didn't want to start our union in debt. Stefano's family were amazing: they all got themselves together, jumped on planes and made it to Liverpool from Rome. We sprung for his dad's hotel room – it was the least we could do – and all my family had to do was drive down the motorway and stay in the small but adequate family home. James came all the way from California to be my man of honour; he wanted to be called maid of honour, but I wouldn't let him, the saucy sod. But what a mate he has turned out to be. As the saying goes, "friends are the family you choose yourself".

Another dear friend Rosemary and her husband Steve also came all the way from California. I went to their wedding with James on my way to the airport as I left America, and it was literally my last stop, so they returned the favour. We ended up having people from all over the globe. I was very touched by this, and very grateful that I had gone for real friends and relatives rather than the showbiz crowd.

Alyn Waterman, my makeup artist from Footballers' Wives, surprised me by bringing his expertise and excitement to me as a gift for my big day and Russell Blackburn from Blackburn Bridal Couture in London gave me a beautiful couture gown and veil that were worth thousands. I felt a million dollars in it. Stefano's Aunty Bila took our photographs – 1,200, if you please – and prepared the wedding album of a lifetime.

The Sunday Mirror did a piece on my preparations. I didn't let them into the wedding because I was bricking it, and I couldn't deal with what might happen. In actual fact, my clan were on their best behaviour. No-one got bladdered before the speeches, which was my second-greatest fear. The first, of course, was the police breaking into the proceedings to cart my brother off to jail. I had many sleepless nights about that one, but fortunately that didn't happen either. Phew!

What did happen was grace, beauty, peace and fun. We had a right laugh and everybody looked great: all the ladies in their 1920s-inspired clothing; my nephew in a purple zoot suit; my brother and his four sons in morning suits we had hired. I even joked in my speech about the fact that all the Oruches were together and that there was no fighting. The peace, though, was short-lived. I love seeing my family so well turned out. That was a precious moment.

We sneaked off on our honeymoon Stefano took me out fishing with the local fishermen in Lamu, off the coast of Kenya. What an experience! What a day! We had to catch our own dinner; thankfully the fishermen caught an abundance and were kind enough to share their catch with us. We drummed and sang songs all the way home.

I married a marine biologist so there is a recurrent theme of water in our lives! After I met Stefano we went to ten countries in fifteen months; he is quite an adventurer. Besides Lamu, we travelled to Australia, California, South Africa, Helsinki, the Azores and all over Italy. We want to, and have started to, see the world together.

We went out on a romantic date by boat in the pitch black, as this was the only way to get from Shela to Lamu. There were multitudes of stars, but I can't say whether I was more terrified or romanced! Every day is an adventure with my husband.

Chapter Seventeen: Honeymoon baby

By the time Stefano and I got back from Lamu, the ceasefire was forgotten and the war games had begun. I brought my brother's dog back from Liverpool because we were counting the days before he was picked back up by the police for breaking the conditions of his parole. I wanted to make sure she was safe. Silly me, I should know better, but I was loved up and wanted to help. I love dogs and used to have a doggy day care business in LA, so she was no trouble for me.

Stefano wasn't convinced, though. Unfortunately, she had stayed with us during burglary season and had killed a cat and a fox so, being so genteel, he wanted nothing more to do with her (despite having initially loved her). I had to argue with him about it, and finally he relented. James was staying with us for a couple of days before heading back to the States and the plan was simple: my mother or sister would pick up the dog from James when they got back to London. They would then care for her while I was on my honeymoon for two weeks – how hard could it be?

Apparently, very. My sister left the dog at mine, pooping up the yard. She also claimed that was what I wanted or that I had forgotten to give her a key to the yard so she couldn't get in to let the dog out. She occasionally went round to feed it, climbing over my security fence. So how secure does my house look if an out-of-shape, forty-five-year-old woman can scale the fence? How convincing are the lights that I have on timers proving that we were home even though the car hadn't moved for days? I was furious! I came back and stayed in London for a few weeks, then packed my car so I could drive to Dublin to be with my husband. The dog was supposed to come with us, but after I packed my new life into the car she didn't fit. So I figured the dog would be safe at my mother's house. Based on the dog's track record I told my sister to get a muzzle for £12.99 from down the street. Again, how hard could it be? She was just too disorganised. I was supposed to come and get the dog three weeks later, but in the interim I had planned to come home from the wedding and carry on as if nothing had happened. About four days after we returned, Stefano went back to work in Ireland, and my cousin Thelma (Pee's sister) came to London to stay with my mother. She is awesome; I love this woman. She said in Nigerian pidgin: "Ah, ah, where is your husband now? What are you doing here? Do you want some other woman to take him? Get your things packed!" I was shocked at my own stupidity. People had asked us for a year where we were going to live and since I had such a beautiful home in the UK and a career forming, I assumed it would be there. But Stef also had a job in Ireland, so we would dodge the question and say, "oh don't go there".

We didn't go there and all of a sudden I was married and living separately from my man. Honey, my older siblings never stayed in the same residence as their respective partners full time, and my mother has never lived with a man permanently in my memory, so I was just acting out what I had seen. Plus I was in denial that the season had shifted because I didn't want anything to change.

However, my cousin had me on the next ship. Thank God for her. When we arrived in Ireland I suddenly noticed that my monthly visitor was late and on taking some tests, I found out I was pregnant. I was having a honeymoon baby! Yes, the Italian had shot and scored! We were elated, but Stefano was very clear: there was to be no dog. My sister continued her madness, claiming the dog had bitten her kid. If that were true the child would be dead, as the dog was ferocious, but she whipped everyone into a frenzy thinking it was true. When I called my mother to tell her my news my sister broke into the conversation and said her drunken husband was "gonna kick my behind if I was ever in LA".

God said this about marriage: "A man shall leave his father and mother and be joined to his wife, and they shall become one flesh" (Genesis 2:24). This is often easier said than done. The problem is, a lot of people standing up there at the altar taking those vows haven't really realised what they're promising. Marriage means all your other relationships (except your relationship with God), now come after your relationship with your wife or husband. Marriage isn't about making space for someone else in your life; it's about rebuilding your life around them.

Here's another thought. When you read the story of Adam and Eve in the book of Genesis, Eve was specially created because Adam really needed her; he couldn't do it on his own, he was incomplete. Think about this: unless a person has found someone to whom they can say, 'I'm incomplete without you', they're probably not ready for marriage. Marriage is a huge decision, so don't rush into it through a fog of passion. Allow God to transform your heart every day into the kind of heart that can offer the love your partner will need from you to make them complete.

I don't think deep down I realised all these things when I got married, even after all the pre-marriage counselling we got from my pastor. These were changes I had prayed for and wanted, but here I was resisting them, feeling as though I was being controlled because I had never had a serious, well-balanced relationship with someone who was my equal before. That's how it was with Stefano.

The pastor had asked me whether I wanted a career with a marriage on the side, and I was so tempted to say yes, but of course I said all the right things. Walking it out though, and putting Stef's needs before my own (or not to sound more sacrificial than I am, even considering he had needs) was not something that came easily for me. We were raised to get as much out of a situation as possible, so giving was something I had to learn to do. I didn't trust anyone to take care of me either. I didn't have examples of many people who were willing to put my needs first, so it was destined to be a bumpy ride.

I came home to deal with my home and to do a TV appearance. I got dropped at my house in a limousine and, as the car pulled up beside my vintage Mini Cooper, two scallies who were trying to rob it jumped out. I was pregnant, freaked out and alone. I really didn't need this! I opened my gate and noticed I had been broken into. The doghouse, of all things, had been taken, and I was fed up. After a sleepless night I smelt my sister's involvement.

I had been carrying my baby for 37 weeks, and that was full term as far as I was concerned. But people laughed at me in the street and gleefully told me: "You're nowhere near the end; first pregnancies usually go to 42 weeks". That meant five more weeks – I did not want to hear that! I couldn't walk, I had destroyed my back, my stomach had stretched to fifty-six inches, I had gone from my usual size eight to struggling to fasten a size fourteen and I had probably put on four stone at a conservative estimate. I say estimate, because after a while I couldn't bear to deal with scales any more, or fight with my husband when he saw his former model wife overly bloated and eyeing another pregnancy craving: a man-sized serving of curry, chips and big fat sausages, which is exactly what my legs had become! I was constantly starving and the notion of five more weeks was more than I could bear.

My mate Anna had given birth on the Saturday and we had the same due date (May 30), but she had gone three weeks early. I had seen her the day before and was mortified to see that we had started out with the same build and I was a little larger than her, even though she was carrying twins.

I had endured Carpal Tunnel Syndrome from sixteen weeks because of all the fluid retention, so I basically couldn't use my hands. I couldn't even get dressed unaided and I couldn't hold onto anything. My husband and I were down to one glass in the house because I'd broken so many, so at mealtimes he would hold the one glass we had left to my lips, allowing me to quench me thirst, but not to drown my sorrows. It was a miserable affair.

We hoped giving birth would give me the use of my hands back. I wanted this baby out!

I did what any rational woman would do. Did I consult God? No. Jesus? No. The oracle? Yes, I turned to Google and the general consensus was castor oil. It said the worst thing that would happen was that you would get diarrhoea and a stomach ache if you weren't ready to give birth. So I decided to listen to what the old wives were telling me and got on the castor oil. I was petrified because I really didn't know what I was doing, but I also was desperate with a capital 'D'.

As soon as my husband went out to work I waddled to the nearest pharmacy; usually a five minute walk, but at this point it took me twenty. I asked for castor oil and sat on a chair in a way that assured the woman I wouldn't budge until I got some. The pharmacist smiled at me knowingly and said she didn't have any. I wept. "What about cod liver oil?" I asked. Now we had never even spoken about what I wanted it for, but she was a pharmacist, so she knew. She said: "No, you need castor oil to induce… Stay there… Stay sat… I'll help you." God love her, she then got on the phone and rang several pharmacies in the area and managed to find me some. I 'jumped' into a taxi, but when I waddled into the pharmacy a tiny Chinese woman, one of those steel magnolia types, brought it out to me. She handed it to me but at the same time wouldn't quite let go. "What you want it for?" she asked. "None of your business!" I said.

We ended up in a tug of war for that bottle. She wanted to sell it to me but was scared it would hurt me and my unborn child. She repeated her question, and I repeated my answer. She finally conceded and I got back in the cab. But then I panicked. What if I was doing something irreversibly stupid; something that would harm my child? But I had already asked the midwife the day before if it worked and she had said that if you were ready it could bring on labour. If you weren't it wouldn't, and you would end up on the toilet.

I took a small sip at first, probably a teaspoon-sized sip. Then I waited about thirty minutes and there was a slight gurgle in the nether regions. I started to get a little strange in the stomach, so I thought "this could be it". So I took a bigger gulp, although it tasted absolutely disgusting. There was more internal quaking and in my insanity I felt I was really onto something until I had to leg it to the bathroom! Fortunately it was close by because I was a little too large to be legging it.

And bingo, I got just what I deserved. I ended up on the toilet all day long! I decided right then that I would keep my first secret from my husband and not tell him. He's a worrier and would not have gone for that tale one bit. I spent the rest of the day fatigued from the effort and was relaying the tale to my friend Tanya on the phone when I felt a tiny trickle. It was innocuous enough, but I knew immediately that my waters had broken, even though it's nothing like the Niagara Falls opus they depict on TV. I said to her calmly: "I have to go, my waters have broken." I said it so calmly, in fact, that after we hung up she called back and said: "Did you just say what I think you did?"

I decided not to call my husband and tell him because he had just texted me to say he was on his way home. I knew that if I called him in traffic, the terror, madness and excitement might lead to a traffic accident. The joke had consistently been that he would probably faint during delivery and have all the nurses care for him instead of me. So I stayed in the upstairs bedroom and waited. I saw him pulling into the driveway about ten minutes later, so I said calmly out of the window: "My waters have broken". if you had seen the look on his face you would know the wisdom of my earlier decision not to tell him.

Thus the journey into motherhood began. I had intermittent contractions all day and my midwife had told me to come into the hospital to have foetal monitoring. I, of course, wanted to know if the baby was alright more than she did. The result was that I was OK and my baby was OK, but despite the 'contractions' I was not actually in labour. But now, because of the waters breaking, I had to have the baby out of me in under thirty-six hours because he was no longer in a sealed womb and was at risk of infection. Well done, Phi! Nice one.

I had planned to have a natural birth, and poor Stefano had indulged my insanity by writing a birth plan that included birthing pools and looking into this strange thing called hypnobirthing. He had spent a small fortune getting me these hypnobirthing sessions from some hack. These people stood around with their hands outstretched from the second I said "I will" when you get engaged, "I do" at the wedding and right through the pregnancy to the birth.

As far as I'm concerned, they were just waiting to exploit how out of your depth and vulnerable you felt by helping themselves to your wallet. For example, a chiropractor recommended a hand massage to relieve the crippling symptoms of Carpal Tunnel Syndrome, but I begged her before she started not to mess with me. At that point I was wearing splints on both wrists and couldn't sleep at night. She squirted a bit of cream on my hands, did sweet FA and charged me eighty euro. Charming!

Anyway, I had told him many times that I didn't want an epidural. I was frightened after hearing a rumour that you could suffer paralysis in the nerves in your back. I told Stefano: "Epidural under no circumstances." I was going to hypnobirth the baby out and possibly sing Kum By Ya afterwards. My sister-in-law said I was mad and I was annoyed at the time, but she was right.

It was a very funny, sweet time after that. My husband and I walked around Dublin with me trying not to throw a temper tantrum because I actually didn't want to walk. I wanted to lie down and eat bonbons! Despite all the myths, hot sex, hot curries and hot walks do nothing to bring on labour. Anyway, we were in a restaurant eating Thai food, when I suddenly told my husband to go and get the car. He said, "Phi, it's a fifteen-minute walk to the house, it will be good for you." I barked: "Now!" He finally understood what was happening, rushed off to get the car and sped me away to hospital.

When I walked up the stairs of the hospital I was all drama. They were trying to get me to walk three feet from the door into the administrator's room so I could be checked in, but I burst into tears: "I can't! It hurts!" So they checked me in from a distance while I cried and my teeth chattered. Then we went into a room to hook me up to a monitor and they told me the baby's heart rate had risen dramatically. He was in distress and I needed an immediate caesarean.

The nurse said: "We need to cut it out," and I quipped: "You will be in distress if you cut anything out of me!" Having seen me on reality TV, she panicked and sent in a heavy: the lead consultant who I had never met. I explained that I was frightened of being cut, but that I certainly wasn't threatening the nurse; I had bigger fish to fry. The doctor was literally dancing with excitement next to the bed, and said: "Don't worry Phina, you won't be cut. How would that look in your next show?"

What planet was I on? What's the matter with people? At a certain point the power of TV and the celebrity culture does your head in and needs to stop! I was terrified of these strange women. And then when they started to induce me, despite all that check-in drama, I wasn't even in labour! Well! Something hurt, but it could have been in my imagination. I was huffing and puffing and crying and carrying on, but as soon as I realised I wasn't in labour the pain miraculously stopped.

While I was waiting to dilate, I was told if I had not dilated by the next morning they would be doing a caesarean. I really feel for women who don't have faith, because I realised they wanted me to have a caesarean so they could schedule what time I gave birth; they can't do that if nature is allowed to run its course. By now I had barked for painkillers and they initially gave me gas and air. But suffering the indignity of being prostate over a birthing ball with just my top on and my bits out for all the world to see, I needed the heavy guns; mainly to deal with the mortification. So I asked for an epidural.

My husband said: "But Phi, I thought you wanted to do it naturally." I gave him a look that would have left my baby fatherless had he seen it. The sergeant major midwife was like: "Let me see if you can have some; it might be too late." Honey, she got the look too, so I was epiduralled to the point where my legs were like a pair of sausages, dead on the bed. I had no feeling in them whatsoever and I wondered how was I going to push this child out. Stef stayed with me and started massaging my legs back to life, what a stud. Sergeant major kept checking on me through the night to see if I was dilated. The other midwife affectionately known as 'nurse cuts' went on her break and in walks this Nigerian woman I had never seen before. She noticed my husband and started speaking to him in fluent Italian. Get this, she was a nun who had been placed at the Vatican, a stone's throw from where Stef grew up. God is so funny! The two of us started to pray. In fact, we prayed all the way through the break, so when the midwife was due to return it coincided with her time to clock off, and instead I was to get another member of the team. Oh joy!

Fortunately, my favourite midwife Fiona from the Community Midwives' Scheme we were part of came on shift. And when the sergeant major next checked on me I had gone from one centimetre to nine centimetres. They both wondered what I had been doing! Fiona was a fun woman. She came back in and said: "You're ready, but I'm just going to have a cup of tea. It's my break time." I love that woman, but I was fuming. However, I now believe with all my heart that she did it on purpose because we had spent a lot of time together and she knew me. When she came back, my outrage worked in my favour, as she had known it would. I wondered why they looked so shocked after the first two pushes and whispered to one another "she's doing really well". I thought they were doing the usual coaching thing, I didn't feel like I was doing really well. I couldn't feel anything apart from my face, which wasn't helped by the epidural. I felt like my head was going to rip off my neck and fall like two slabs of meat onto the floor.

On the third push he crowned and came out. He was gorgeous! Ok, I'm lying, he was blue with a pointy head! He had slanty eyes, no eyelashes and loads of dark curls on his head. That was not what I was expecting! He looked a bit like Dan Ackroyd in the Cone Heads and he was doing Matrix-style moves with his arms and legs. I loved him instantly! They gave him to me and put him under my top, and he nursed immediately and regained his colour, turning from blue to alabaster white. Funny, greedy little thing. He's still the same today: a little darker, but not much. I love him more my than my own breath.

I had false eyelashes and my hair curled to go out to dinner with my husband, which was where I had been when all the palaver started. So I gave birth looking like a character from a TV show. My husband and I still roll about laughing when we think about it. Also, ten minutes after I gave birth the cheeky midwife asked if the antenatal class could come in and ask us questions about it because we looked so good. It was good PR for the Community Midwives' Scheme at the hospital!

Paolo had lost his blue colour, and his pointy head was covered with a nice little hat; he was wrapped up like a burrito. Stef's a lecturer, and I'm a drama queen so we said "sure". The eight or nine women came in with huge eyes and their husbands and birthing partners looked on intently. Remember, I was all glammed up and the birth, though induced, was easy. There were just seventeen minutes from full dilation to him taking his first feed.

My husband was very emotional and I was very self-deprecating and funny, but when Paolo cooed he brought down the house. He's been stealing my thunder ever since! The couples left with a really false sense of how it would go for them, but I thought it was kinder really. If I had been on the ball I might have acted out a three-act play – screaming, crying with pain, drenched and shivering – and scared them witless!

Since my husband had been up all night and mother and baby were fine, it was suggested that Stef go home to sleep. They wheeled me into a recovery ward where there were six other bundles of joy and six happy customers. The babies were all squawking, but mine was angelic in his silence. I remember thinking smugly how easy he was and how awfully noisy those "other" babies were. Later I learned that he had just been resting.

Once they had drawn the curtain around us I was on the bed like a beached whale, popping pills like a maniac. I was happy that I had an excuse to because in a normal day I don't medicate pain; I think it's useful because it makes you pay attention. Pao was in his little clear

Perspex cot and suddenly he made this little "mew" like a kitten. It was almost inaudible and I was suddenly aware that I hadn't a clue what to do! My God, you had to have a license for a dog and a TV, but they just let you walk out of the hospital with a baby after a few paltry classes. Oh my!

My mum wasn't there as we knew she would distress me, and my sisters weren't talking to me, surprise surprise. My husband was at home and it suddenly dawned on me that I was this little boy's survival strategy. Honey, I shrieked in horror then very quickly pushed the call button. I needed some help, now! Another of the midwives I got on really well with came by and I told her he was "mewing". She laughed kindly and told me to pick him up because he was lonely. So with fear in my heart, both at the newness of his precious life and the Carpal Tunnel making me very clumsy, I did just that.

On his first day in a sweater his nonna (Italian for nanny) made him. I couldn't stop looking at his cheeks! This was during the phase when he slept around the clock and was very quiet because, like I said, he was resting. He found his lungs on the third night. I woke up to the sound of vomiting and crying. The vomiting was Stef through pure exhaustion and the crying was the baby because he didn't know where I was. I had put him in his Moses basket because I lived in fear of rolling over him in my sleep; such is the intensity of the tiredness you feel in that season.

I crawled from the bed. Why was I crawling? I'm so glad you asked! The epidural did exactly what I had feared it would do and left me unable to stand up straight or walk without a cane for weeks. As I crawled through the bedroom on all fours, I suddenly remembered what my pastor had said: "With marriage and a baby your life changes forever." It was quicker than lightning!

Chapter Eighteen: Rebirth

Old habits die hard, and soon after I had the baby and got settled down I became restless. I wanted to be back in the world of acting, back in the spotlight. I don't live comfortably in my own skin on a daily basis, and I was tired all the time, which isn't surprising. But I was also bored. Creatives create good things, or they create drama.

Being a mummy did a lot to reveal my brokenness afresh. First of all, my son is perfect and I don't mean that in the general psycho mother way, where your kid is the only thing you can see. I mean apart from his physical beauty and his very sweet spirit. He hadn't had a chance to mess up or to be anything other than what God had created him to be. But that didn't mean that he just came out, I accepted him and everything was perfect. I wish.

He had an instant and insatiable need for food. There's nothing strange there and I had an abundant supply. He had a need to be clothed, clean and dry, no problem there either. He was very sleepy and a ball of beautiful smells and cuddles, which was amazing. But I wasn't prepared for the sacrificial element, the relentlessness, or what a lack of sleep can do to a couple who have only been married nine months.

I wasn't prepared to sacrifice what I normally did either, it was a very steep learning curve. Fortunately, the love was there instantly; however, that little perfect guy was like a highlighter for my character deficiencies and imperfections. Thank the Lord that my baby and my sweet husband were able to love me anyway. I fretted, cried frustration, mourned my old life and – dare I say it – my old body.

All the things I thought about stay-at-home mums came largely from my experiences with my own mother. Because mothering cost my dear mum so much, I wasn't into the idea of being someone's mum. All that garbage came out to get me, especially since, from time to time, people would inquire about my career and when the next major role would happen.

Also, for the first time in my life, I had major body issues. After all my pontificating about natural births and hypnobirth, I fell before I hit the first hurdle. At the mere suggestion of pain I was screaming out for an epidural, which reduced me to a slab of beef lying on the table. Then I didn't have any pain to caution me, so when I pushed, I did potentially irreparable damage to my stomach muscles and lower back, which had not been particularly strong in the first place because of all the twists and turns the early gymnastic training had done to my lower spine.

So because I'm quite fit and did yoga all the way through my pregnancy, I wasn't prepared for my body to not respond in the way I expected it to. This wasn't merely a vanity issue: for a couple of months after the birth I wasn't always certain I would be able to stand or walk. It was quite terrifying, actually.

I had always had the African sway back, a dip in the spine, and some junk in my trunk, which created a little pot belly. Since my early modelling days I had always been told to breathe in, which is cute at fifteen and maybe even at twenty-five, because you have the youth to carry it off. But now it's just a sad reminder that my back is messed up. Also, my hands still weren't working because of the Carpal Tunnel. Now how was that going to work? I had no legs to stand on and no hands to hold the baby/ I was a mess!

I tell you what, though, legions of people will prey on you during this time, awaiting your insecurity, vulnerability and weakness of mind. I had never contemplated plastic surgery in my life, but as I checked my email for signs of my former life there were constant adverts showing reality show stars with mega boob implants. They had all been "enhanced" by these butchers, I mean "surgeons". I got obsessed with a new stomach because I hadn't regained the figure I had had before.

Since 2006 I had run five marathon events and half starved in the jungle, so who knew what my real body looked like! Plus I had also been airbrushed to death in magazines a lot of the time, so I was losing the plot. I wanted to look like the girl in the media, but I was drenched in baby sick, had had too many sleepless nights and could hold my stomach in my hand like a designer bag without the coveted label!

So for the first time ever my logic left me. I gave someone £450 to give me about thirty injections in my stomach. The process, called Lipo Dissolve, was supposed to melt away my stomach fat. It should be called Money Dissolve since that's the only thing it melted away. There was this massive disclaimer about the fact that it works on 95% of people. Why? So that when it doesn't work for you (and it won't) they can say that they told you so. Then I got into a long song and dance with the surgeon from the internet ad that I had talked to. It was all about how much publicity they could get for carving me up, and of course they oversold me and told me that even though I only had a little bit of stomach fat (that none of my friends could even see) I now needed a tummy tuck! They wanted my money, my endorsement and to saw me in half leaving a nasty scar! The surgeon even told me that at first I would be bent forward until my stomach muscles stretched. He said all this with a comedic Indian accent and a toupee on his head. He was about the same height as my son, as I looked down to meet his eye and suddenly saw the light. I zipped right down to the lingerie shop and bought a girdle and I have never been happier.

Then I finally did what I should have done in the first place: I went on to get my Yoga Teacher Training Certificate, which had been a long-time goal. Is my stomach still there? I don't know, I'm wearing a girdle (joke). Who even cares if it's still there? If my own pictures can make me feel inadequate then what are all the supermodels' pictures doing to everybody else, I wonder. I finally got my stomach fat down by changing my diet, then Stefano followed suit. For me there were no shortcuts; all my life I had been able to eat like a man and look like a model, but after Paolo my metabolism shifted and whatever I ate stayed on my body.

I would sit with my baby on the couch all day in Dublin, and I started to create a fantasy in my head, you know the one in which the grass is greener. I managed to convince myself that if I went home my little baby and I would be better off. After all, I have two sisters, sometimes a brother, a mother and three or four nephews and nieces in London within a six-mile radius of my front door, and I would be close to my work. I would be able to go to auditions and I would have help on hand.

It took a lot to convince my husband of this but I thought it would be better because I have a lovely house there, with more space. He could come back for weekends and holidays. It was the best of times, it was the worst of times. No family showed up to greet me, which was quite painful, and worse still there was no curiosity about my child. Thank God he was too young to recognise the snub.

The final knockout blow was that no people translated to no help, which we were desperate for. One sister passed the house every day to go to work, but didn't stop by, apart from to ask if I could babysit one of her children since we were home anyway. I saw her plenty when I was being invited everywhere and people were laying on the limousines for me. Even then my mother would say she was coming at 8am and when she rocked up at 4pm, or didn't show at all, she wondered why I was angry.

Being alone with a baby, even one as good and loved as my son, is a mind-wrecker. God created marriage and family for a reason: to protect the women from nearly killing herself trying to do it all. I have read all the unhelpful women's mags and seen all the celebrity magazines featuring the celebs promoting the "I can do it all" fallacy. The headlines reading: "I'm back in my jeans after two weeks" or "How I balance my work with high-profile events and manage to look twenty-five even though I'm thirty-five."

There is a lot of horse crap being sold to people. A lot of women feel like losers because they can't do it all. They don't have the means, the support or the presence of mind… or the makeup artists and special lighting you get on those shoots. I have had it up to the back teeth with the "too posh to push" brigade, who have caesareans and tummy tucks at the same time, or are the same size as they were at seventeen but have a deftly concealed cocaine habit. Then to top off they give out this Celebrity Mother of the Year award. Previous recipients are too terrifying to mention. Who's next, Vanessa George?

What's clear to me it that you can't have it all, so don't make out that you can. Or at least come clean and say: "Yes, I have six children under five but they have a nanny each and I don't see them. I never get up in the middle of the night with them; they're actually in a separate wing of the house." Or: "Yes, I am back in my jeans, but you should see the cosmetic surgery bill." Or: "I haven't had a decent meal since 1982." How funny and liberating that would be for womankind.

How about people telling you beforehand that caring for a baby, though a privilege, is nullifying? It can be soul-destroying and take you straight into meltdown, identity crisis, and post-natal depression. The hours between 5am and 7pm were very, very hard during that period. But however hard they are, if you neglect to put the time in with your children early in their lives, you can be sure you will put more time in on the therapist's couch, or worse.

Make sure you get directions to yummy mummy island quick. I joined a group in the local park in a desperate bid to avoid topping myself. I make light of it now, but in the darkness days of post-natal depression, I couldn't even bath Paolo properly because I couldn't hold him; I still didn't have the use of my hands. I really couldn't bear the thought of living another second and the only reason I didn't end it all is that I wanted my son to be healthy and happy, which (delightfully) he is. Had I have done myself in, I would have ruined his future, leaving him with a weight of guilt that would have driven him mad.

It's tough being on your own with a child when you're up at 6am to go to a 9.30am running class and it's still 50/50 as to whether or not you'll be late. When after running you try to hang out with people until they literally have to peel you off them like a limpet. And when you watch the clock until it is his naptime or bedtime so you can crawl to bed yourself.

That's what that time was like for me. If my son teethed or cried out in the night I was floating on a sea of exhaustion the next day. I texted everyone for help. Myleene was very helpful and always replied. I was with Myleene one day when Paolo projectile vomited everything in his stomach endlessly, and I cried like a wet rag. Having a child thirteen months older, she inducted me into the NHS Direct hall of fame. She is a lovely lady; always sending me cheery texts and answering my mad ones.

The assistant pastor at my church in Dublin had told me to "take my time". I slowly started to remember and heed that advice. It's true, I didn't give myself enough time. The self-pity that took over me when I got back to England was absolutely ridiculous! There are so many women I know that would love to have my son or my husband for that matter, and there I was clinging to old dreams. I wasn't being patient with myself or giving myself the time I needed to nurture the mother that was trying to emerge. Basically, I was making myself miserable.

So I gave it up, postponed my work for a season and went back to Dublin.

Chapter Nineteen: Winds of change

I still have so many questions, but I realise now that I was being given the raw material for all I am today. I wish God had told me earlier everything I have since learned, or given me the blueprint to save my tears, but He didn't. That's why He is God and I, thankfully, am not. That's why I need faith. If you see the glorious ending, what do you need faith for? You need faith when you're eating cereal with water and a dash of sterilised milk, hoping for better days with the telephone and power switched off. Please don't misunderstand me, I'm not bitter. There are two choices when you face adversity: bitter or better. I, by the grace of God, chose better and pray that I will continue to do so. It was and still is a slow process.

I'm writing this for the woman who still finds herself in a bad situation, telling her to hold on. Telling her that if she believes and trusts in Him, God will redeem the time she has 'lost'. Telling her she does not have to act out, or act rough, rude or impossible – I still have to tell myself that too. I don't have to try and fix a spiritual situation with a fleshly answer. No, no, no, baby girl. God has much better plans for you. I know this because He had much better plans for me.

I understand now why I went to America in the first place. I just wanted a chance to excel and do the work I was trained to do, Americans love anyone who dares to step out and try something new; they love the pioneer spirit. Eventually I grew tired of being away from my family, because in truth I had forgotten the extent of the lunacy and asked myself how bad it could really have been. I thought maybe I had overblown the trauma and hilarious tragedy of it all. I hadn't.

You have to be really clever when your ship finally comes in. There were many distractions, always a swirl of parties to attend, so it can be hard to focus. I understand now why some bright young thing breaks out in an extraordinary way and then their work gets steadily more mediocre as each moment passes.

Finding the balance between enjoying your success and being able to go to all the things you had always longed to go to, and not wearing yourself out and rendering yourself useless in the process, is difficult. Sometimes, getting to the next level after a breakthrough is tough too. Sometimes a successful role makes you typecast; sometimes producers think they know too much about you. Sometimes they want a new face and sometimes an absence makes people forget you. It's all bonkers, but so must I be because I love it.

Wednesday January 20, 2010, was my D-Day. It was a day I had haggled and moaned and bullied my husband (as if) to agree that I could return to California to seek my fortune. It was a tense time as I had a 20-month-old son who needed me very much, but I also had excellent childcare and a husband who is an incredible father. So it was finally decided that I would head back to California because there just weren't the work opportunities I needed in Britain, let alone Ireland.

I was enrolled in the local church's School of Ministry, a class that lasted a year, so the other five class members were none too pleased that I was leaving after the first semester. They were polite about it, but there was a sense that I was letting the side down. The assistant pastor gave me a hard time and had a look of disappointment on her face whenever I saw her. But I had been through this before with other churches. They aren't exactly approving of the entertainment industry in the first place, and in the second they prefer that you put the needs of the church before your own. You have to discern for yourself where you want to be: it was a new year and I wanted to try again.

My husband is a civil servant and as a result of the recession, he had received several pay cuts from the Irish government since I started my class. His research money was cut and promotion opportunities were suspended. I actually really wanted to work and, as much as the School of Ministry was filling me up spiritually, I felt I had a larger duty of care to put money into the family budget. This was the longest period in my life that I had not done any significant work. I had done bits and pieces and even had a film, Happy Ever Afters, in the cinema. But I still felt I hadn't played a substantial enough role.

It was the first time I had been taken care of financially, but when the going got tough I wasn't only willing to go back to work, I really wanted to help my beloved. So I bought a few fancy clothes, went on a diet to finally get rid of the baby belly that would not have worked in LA, and bought my ticket. Paolo is very perceptive, so he started crying whenever I left the room and became really clingy. I would say to
Stefano "he knows" but he would say "don't be ridiculous". But thinking about it, he understands everything else we tell him, so obviously my little smart kid was listening in to all our adult conversations and was letting me know loud, and tantrumly clear, what he thought about it.

The Thursday before I was due to leave, my agent called about an audition for a part in Waterloo Rd. Shed, the makers of the programme, had made Footballers' Wives, so I was confident I would get it, especially when I found out the character was called "Adanna", my middle name, and that she was Nigerian. She had to deal with unruly teenagers who came from tough economic and social backgrounds, so I believed with all my heart I'd get the part.

I flew into London and ran into my dear friend Tanya, who was also auditioning for the role. I told her how much I wanted it after we had both read and God bless her she said she hoped I got it. All the while, I was thinking the part had been sent from God so that I didn't have to leave my husband and son to look for work.

I was so in faith about it that I wasn't sure whether to travel to LA. They weren't going to make a decision before I left, and I would have plenty of time to return, but there was an uneasiness in my spirit about going to LA that I couldn't shake. My husband, who isn't a fan of his actress wife's ever-changing mind, said: "Please, Phina, for heaven's sake go". He had been listening to my misery about not working more or less since we met and he knew I thought of LA as the answer to everything acting-related because I had worked there for twelve years as an actress with no problems before. But life had changed, and so had the economy!

I asked my agent to call and check whether there was any further interest in me and she did. It can be the kiss of death to force these people into a decision before they are ready, but after fifteen years as an actress I also knew that if you're not careful, you can sit there waiting, feeling upset and not living your life, and I had been in the game too long for that. So she called and they said there was no further interest in me for the part. Now here's the thing, I didn't believe them! I had such a strong feeling in my spirit that I was to work in Britain, so I ignored it because everybody was telling me it was over.

Nevertheless, I went to the airport on Wednesday morning. I had tried to kiss, cuddle and explain to Paolo that I was going away, but he was too young to get it and was impatient to go with his dad; it was a novelty because usually I took him to nursery. I took a cab to the airport and checked in. By the time I got through all the screening they do and was sitting by the gate, I called my friend and prayer partner to pray these things through. As soon as I spoke to her, the freedom and safety we have in talking about the hard stuff, the fact that we don't wear masks with each other meant I started weeping openly in the airport, I was so sad.

Now it might seem pathetic to someone else. Why, since I had made this choice was I there in the airport blubbering? But that's the thing; I didn't feel I had a choice. Acting jobs in the UK are rare, especially for African actors. I'm very happy to be part of the entertainment industry over here, but you do get pushed to the limits. That's why a lot of our finest actors have emigrated to LA or travel back and forth: they want what they rightfully deserve.

I was texting my British agent with updates of my travel, hoping beyond hope she would say: "Stop! Come back, you've been recalled". But there was nothing apart from her warmest wishes for

LA. I arrived in London Heathrow Terminal 1 and had to wait for my bags, which was tricky because the next flight was in Terminal 3 and departed in fifty minutes. It was a twenty-minute walk away, so I got my bag, took to my heels and sprinted like a loony over to Virgin Atlantic. At first they told me I was too late, but another lady passenger and I pleaded with our eyes, so the desk clerk picked up the phone and asked the baggage handlers if they could take two more.

My mother had told me she would come to see me between flights, but I didn't want her to because she is notoriously late and I didn't want to be waiting for her and miss the flight. As I ran onto the gangplank to board my mother texted me that she was in the airport and in the wrong terminal, God bless her. So I had to tell her I was actually boarding the flight. The disappointment in her voice was a killer.

I watched a few films on board and tried to sleep. I had a very funny Indian travelling companion so the time passed quickly. Soon enough I was with James in the pick-up truck driving in the rain (yes, its rains in LA every January, though no one believes me!) and we were just happy to be together again. I hadn't seen him since my wedding! He drove me to my friend Marty's house, where I had been staying when I originally left for my Footballers' Wives audition and again on my return.

It was quite funny seeing Marty's house again, because though four-and-a-half years had passed, nothing had changed. Even the Do Not Disturb sign lifted from a hotel was still on my bedroom door. We sat catching up, watching films and just generally glad and happy to be together again. I went to the grocery store and filled the fridge, then opened my suitcase and completely unpacked. I have to do that whenever I travel. It helps me feel that I am settled and ready to work, so that when I wake up in the morning I'm ready to hit the ground running.

I texted my husband that I was safe, and finally went to bed about 2am after writing my to-do list for the next day. At 3am the phone rang, and I thought it was my mother or husband checking on me. I desperately hoped it wouldn't wake up the whole household. I realised I had terminated the contract on my Irish phone, so it hadn't delivered the texts but Marty was sleeping on his office floor because his elderly mother was visiting, so I didn't dare go in there to pick up the phone. I just hoped they wouldn't be disturbed.

The next morning at 7am I decided to sneak into the office to get the phone because I figured it was too long for my husband not to have heard from me. I was successfully sneaking back past Marty when he mumbled: "Some lady from England called last night. She said she was your agent and it was urgent." I was so excited I couldn't remember the international dialling code; I kept getting the wrong number.

So I gave the phone to Marty to dial, but my agent's receptionist couldn't hear me and hung up. I tried again but the line rang to voicemail... Aaaaaaaaaaaaaaargggggh! Then the receptionist said she was in the office with a client. I asked her to go and wave the phone under her nose as it was constantly going straight to voicemail.

When my agent finally came on the line, she said: "Hi darling, did you get my email? You need to be in Manchester to screen test for a new character on Coronation Street on Friday afternoon at 4.30pm." I didn't even know what day it was in England or what time is was, or whether my ticket was changeable, or whether a seat would be available. But since I had been praying for a way to stay with my baby, I was sure that this was it.

The next thirty odd hours were bedlam. I printed off the script as I cooked the boys breakfast, mindful of the fact that this was the last time I would see them for a while. Instead of being with them for a couple of months and reinvesting in our friendship I was getting ready to say goodbye to them again. They were alternating between taking the mickey and running lines with me. James actually packed my bag for me and sat on top of it, marvelling at the fact that I could even close the thing.

I also called the London agent to see if the Corrie people could see me on Monday or maybe an hour or so later, to which the answer was an emphatic no; I had the last slot available. I called Virgin Atlantic and several other airlines to see whether or not I could change my ticket. It was possible but there was a change fee and I had to go directly to the airport. Thank God for friends! Both being actors, James and Marty were very supportive. Knowing me and the madness of our profession they never once doubted that I could go and get the part.

So I went off clutching their collective enthusiasm and goodwill. James took me to the nail shop first (I can't act without my claws on!) then to get my brows tweezed (I don't need to explain this!) then to see and explain to my LA agent that, after much fanfare about me finally being able to come to Los Angeles for a serious amount of time so that I could be available to them, I was actually leaving in under twenty-four hours!

Oh, brother. By the time I got there it was lunchtime and my agent had just stepped out to lunch. It had been torrentially raining since my arrival in LA and the news had been full of reports of the terrible weather, so when the assistant called him to come back he wouldn't. In a way I was relieved. The next stop was Toys 'R' Us as I needed to buy a DS game for my six-year-old nephew that I hadn't sent for Christmas. This was followed by a very surreal entrance into his primary school class, where he was so excited by the gift he promptly turned his back on me to get on and play with it. Then I finally to the airport, where my excess baggage caught up with me. I had to pay hefty fines for my packing sins.

Flight 008 left at 6pm LA time and got into Heathrow Terminal 3 at 12.30pm. My sweet agent had sent me an email saying:

Hi Phina

Hope you're not too stressed.

You are booked onto the British Airways flight BA 1394 it departs terminal 5 at Heathrow at 13.40 so you need to be at the gate for boarding at 13.10

you will arrive at Manchester terminal 3 where I have booked you a car to pick you up at 14.40 they will meet you the arrivals gate, they will have a board with your name on it. the drivers number is xxxxxxxxxxx

you will be going to Granada TV 4th Floor Quay Street Manchester the cab will be £25

Emma or I will check you onto the flight in the morning with Claire our travel agent.

Good Luck

Tara

So let's get this straight: I had fifty minutes to get on the flight to Manchester. I knew from the previous day that the luggage carousel can take fifty minutes to even move, so I had to have faith in the Lord that even though it was impossible for man, nothing is impossible for God.

I asked the lovely stewardesses if they could find me a seat further forward on the plane, and God bless them they did, but it meant I was in an exit row and had to learn the procedure to open the plane door. I was sitting next to a chatty South African guy; there always seems to be a chatty person when you have a script in your hand. People always want to know what they might have seen you in. Acting and modelling are the only professions where, if you're not famous, you get tortured by people wanting you to list your credits. Then they always pretend they have seen you on TV. I told him really nicely that I didn't have time to talk, but he was offended.

It was a long, restless flight of me murmuring the lines to myself like a looper and trying to sleep, alternating between thinking I had it nailed and asking the stewardesses if they could help me on the ground. They had told me that the flight was going to get in early at 12.15pm, and true to form at 12pm the captain started getting us ready to land. One of the stewardesses, who I had spoken to extensively about my need, had promised that before the captain switched off the seatbelt sign she would hustle me to the front.

All of a sudden a lady who I had helped on with her baby ten hours earlier said: "It's quarter to one". For some reason we were stacked in the air and no-one had said a word. Finally the seat belt sign pinged and the stewardess brought me forward. The doors opened and I decided to leave my bag on the carousel and just leg it for a bus to the other terminal. It took ten minutes for the bus to come and ten minutes to get there. Then I was running up the gangplank in Terminal Five saying I had a tight connection. The British Airways flight connections lady smiled and said: "No dear, you've missed the flight."

There was another flight I could be booked on for another sixty quid. She took me into the booking office and it was about this time that I realised I had no mobile. My Irish one had been turned off and my British one was dead as a doornail because it was never used. I needed to speak to my agent to see whether or not it was worth getting the ticket seeing as it would get in too late for the appointment I had been given.

One member of the BA ticketing staff was a dead ringer for Ed Harris. He was an interesting man with a very severe twitch, which I had to pretend not to notice. I walked up to him like a gunslinger or a hoodlum from a movie and said: "I need your phone…now." God bless him, he dialled the number and gave it to me, and waited on the line while I discovered my fate. I figured that God would come through. But then my inner demons started taunting me, telling me what a loony I was; that I had made a mistake and was wasting my time; that I had lost everything, the trip to LA, the ticket home and the audition. I kept hearing in my mind how I was too greedy. Then I heard four magical words: "You have until 6pm."

Then I felt happy and confident. I knew the Lord was with me, and I was able to go into the bathroom, change into my costume and redo my hair and make-up. I even had time to listen to some gospel because I had got to the point in the script where I had overworked it and couldn't take it in any more.

When I got out of the bathroom all the men in the terminal seemed to be eating me with their eyes. I wondered whether I had gone too far with the clothing. I only put on a little black dress and fishnet tights, pushed up my cleavage and pumped my hair, but it shows how different my life was at that point. I used to dress like that all the time, but by this point I was a jeans and t-shirt mum. My flashiest accessory was a toddler clinging to my side like a koala bear.

I sat between two Mancunian men on the 35-minute flight and was able to ask them lots of questions about the distance I had left to travel. Should I take a taxi or the train? And most important of all, did I look like a hooker? Why were all the men staring at me? They kindly replied that it was because I looked good. It turned out the older guy was an avid Corrie fan; a veritable almanac. He told me: "If you're late, tell them they should have sent Lloyd to pick you up in his taxi!"

I was reading with Lloyd so it was good to get a substantial character breakdown from this guy and ask lots of questions. As with Footballers' Wives, which I didn't watch prior to joining the cast, I never watched Corrie, so it was new territory for me. I was raised on it as a girl: who can forget Hilda Ogden, Vera Duckworth and Bet Lynch? I was reared on those strong, funny women, but since I had taken to globetrotting, working as an actress myself and becoming a mother, I hadn't had much opportunity to check back in with it.

Ironically, though, when I first came back to Britain, I was asked to present with Steve Macdonald on An Audience with Coronation Street when Johnnie Briggs (Mike Baldwin) retired. So I knew that I had favour and was at least known to someone in management; providing they hadn't had a clean sweep of the house, which sometimes happens. I arrived at Manchester Airport and the stewardesses let me off first. The taxi was there waiting for me and we raced down a traffic-free road, which he seemed very surprised at since it was 4.30pm. It was a miracle.

The cabbie wanted to be chatty too, but since his phone was ringing off the hook with agents, assistants and producers checking on my whereabouts, it was easy to explain that this was not a moment when I could talk freely. I spoke to my agent and asked what a screen test was. I thought I knew, but it was better to be safe than assume anything! She said: "Oh, that's when you go onto the set and shoot with the actor as if you were doing a day's work." I asked if I could use the script and she said: "No darling, it's assumed you are beyond that." At this point I was fatigued and my brain didn't feel like I could remember my name, never mind the scene. Oh Lord!

I got hustled towards the set in a blur of assistants and walked the famous cobbles! When I saw the Rovers Return, I was absolutely gobsmacked at the effect it all had on me! I had to ask the assistant to give me a minute to compose myself, which he very kindly did. About five minutes later I was in bed with Lloyd shooting a scene for Coronation Street! Wow.

As quickly as it started it was finished, and I politely said goodbye to Craig, Kim and June. But now I had the small problem of my luggage being at Heathrow and not having a ticket home. I had no brain cells left and hadn't had any sleep for the last 48 hours. All of a sudden I was mind-numbingly tired.

Considering I had been heading for Los Angeles, it would be fair to say there is truth in the adage: "Want to make God laugh? Show Him your plans". I didn't get the part, but I loved the journey, and I love the fact that you cannot get ahead of God. It felt exactly like what happened with Footballers' Wives, so I was sure it was going to happen.

But God works in different ways every time, and there I was thinking I had Him pegged. The mad thing is, even knowing the results I would make the exact same call today. The wonderful thing is I got to be home with my Italian boys. As far as acting roles go, whatever is mine won't pass me by. They never have before.

Chapter Twenty: A work in progress

I used to think that I had been victorious by just surviving my childhood and being able to cover it up with achievements, but the applause was hollow. I'd got to the point where people kept telling me I had lost my ambition, my drive, or that I didn't do enough with my "celebrity" status and the opportunities it afforded me. One of my sisters even offered to manage my career! But as I look at people who are further along that road, and the pressure that comes with that world, I know I made the right choices at that time. That doesn't change the fact that I love to act and will always strive to do so.

Naturally, when my child is settled in school I will resume my career; I just don't know what direction it will take. Learning to mind my own business and not get distracted by the things that have distracted me in the past is a constant battle. Am I my brother's keeper? In short, no! He was constantly on my mind and I worried and fretted about him to a point that wasn't healthy for either of us. I maintain that I would not be who I am today without my mother, father, brother and sisters, so I'm grateful to them. But I need to remain free of the old, negative thought patterns so I don't carry anyone mentally anymore; not one more step. Freedom is assured if I'm able to do that consistently. Whenever I have managed to do that, I have, by the grace of God, been successful.

You could ask why we have to go through anything. People have and will go through things that are much more painful than anything I've been through or could describe in this book. I guess the question is, why? I want to know, as much as you do why such atrocities happen. I recently learned that after winning her battle with breast cancer, my lovely Roxanna died because the chemotherapy left her immune system so weak. Why?! Why do people go through such tremendous hurt, pain and rejection? I know from speaking to many people that these questions cannot be answered. This stops many people from trusting and believing in God and I can empathise with that.

This is certainly the case for those that have been orphaned, widowed, lost a child or are gripped with fear because of financial meltdown. If you have put your faith in man, coin or institution and you're left with nothing: I understand. I had always put my faith in what I could create with my hands. And in the end my work took me from the pit – the lowest of the low – to the palace, both financially and literally.

However, earthly kingdoms cannot be relied upon. I've had as many, if not more, lows post-success than I ever had before it. I giggle now at my naivety, thinking that I controlled anything, and that I could save myself through the sheer work of my hands. Don't misunderstand me, I'm not saying that you shouldn't work hard; you absolutely should and God commends that. What you shouldn't do is think that money, power or popularity will take you where you ultimately need to go. We have lost a number of bright shining talents over the last few years. I was saddened by the deaths of Michael Jackson, Amy Winehouse and Whitney Houston: each had the world at their feet and still it wasn't enough. I relate to that, but I'm convinced that there is something more substantial than this seemingly fabulous stuff.

I always have to be reminded that I need grace that is sufficient for each day; there are certain things that I know nothing about and cannot predict. It probably sounds really straightforward, but the work of the believer is simply to believe. That's where I started, with a tiny bit of belief. Have you noticed that countries that are incredibly poor are normally very open to God and His ways? We who are so developed, so sophisticated, pooh pooh of all that because we are so connected. But what are we connected to?

We have our BlackBerrys, computers, games, radios and iPods. We work sixty-hour weeks and have the television blaring adverts at us, and we wonder why we can't hear ourselves think; why we can't find our true selves or destinies. We are often distracted by these things, but deep down we have the same issues. It's a malady known as the human condition.

I'm just so glad God loved me enough to save me and shield me from bad behaviour, including my own. People say: "God loves you just as you are, but he loves you too much to leave you that way." I can relate to that. I can't control anything but myself, so that's my goal; to be able to say I've lived in a way that is pleasing to God and those who my life directly affects at the end of each day.

My child is the only one I keep in my mind constantly, and strive to influence and encourage. When he is able to reason, to think for himself and to be independent, I want to be proud of him, and naturally I want him to be respectful and proud of me. That means I have to live in a way that doesn't give him any cause to be ashamed.

My goals at present are very simple: to be a good mother, a good wife and a trusted friend. To multiply and make use of my talents in the right season, acting, writing, painting and hopefully directing. To be used to minister hope to the broken-hearted, especially young women, and to be happy no matter where I am on the planet. I want to stop looking for validation from the outside and assessing my viability based on what I have produced in the last calendar year.

I've got my hands full now and am building a healthy family structure with my boys, having dinners and family gatherings with the little one and all his friends. Family is central. I need to have balance: all family and no work wasn't right for me and all work and no family wasn't either. Something about motherhood and Stefano's calming influence has given me the courage to look at my imperfections and my family relationships, and to decide that I love them all. But the Bible says you must leave your family and cleave unto your husband. That's what I'm doing now and I'm having a ball.

I noticed that in the past I have completely abandoned myself and my dreams in order to be loved, because that's what I was trained to do. The myth is that if you are smaller and less threatening, you'll be easier to love. Well that's just nonsense. We are called to live to our full capacity. I'm an adult now and I'm choosing a different way and a different type of person to create a life with. I have challenged that old notion and am walking the path God has for me.

I have walked away from a plethora of things, always trying to keep the secret insanity away from the public eye. I can't believe I've only just considered giving up running away! I don't have to fear anyone anymore; I can have a happy life. I choose to be very selective about who I spend time with and what I choose to do for work these days. I can act, paint, write, sing and dance and I'm very grateful that I have gone into a deeper period of personal, spiritual and creative recovery. There is a lot to recover from and I'm blessed to be doing it: reading the Word, building myself back up and making plans.

Instead of "thick-lipped, ugly bitch" in my mind I have learned to meditate on the following so it will manifest in my life: "I am emotionally secure, I am financially secure. I am strong, I am healthy, I am whole, I am prosperous. I am complete. I am a wonderful mother, a faithful wife and a Proverbs 31 woman. Physically, emotionally, mentally and spiritually there is nothing broken, nothing missing. My heart is enlarged. I am growing in wisdom, every day in every way." Another good one is: "I am able to balance motherhood and love with fulfilling, lucrative creative work in the fields of acting and directing. I am able to thrive not survive and I have a new, very supportive, family."

I am learning Italian in order to deepen my relationship with Stefano's relatives and I have wonderful friends the world over. I don't need to go back to old, unsavoury relationships because I am very blessed and hardworking. Perhaps that blessing has been there because I've had such a difficult passage. If you've had very shaking beginnings, it's time to really count your blessings and stop dwelling on the negatives. What have you got to lose? Old habits die hard; if you fall back into negative thoughts, meditate on God's Word and start thinking about something better.

Stefano and I are living our lives together as we should: that's why we got married. He is an amazing man, father, lover and friend. Paolo matters more to me than anything I have ever created or ever will create, so I can't have anything making me crazy again. I won't give into my old need to be "famous" again by tomorrow night. I am very happy; my life is colourful and wonderful and I now have nothing to prove.

They say that forty is when life begins; I'm prepared to act now in order to fulfil that. It's also amazing when you have to immediately choose to trust God and not to lean on your own understanding but to acknowledge Him in all your ways so that He can direct your path. You don't need anybody to support your dream peripherally. Obviously, it's nice if you have that, but don't give up if you don't. You need to petition God. He stripped me of the fake identity of fame and false friends; it's worth remembering that anyone can leave you, but God never will.

I not only a father now in the form of my father-in-law, who is amazing to me, but I have a father for my child and a heavenly Father. So I have gone from being fatherless to fatherfull, which, for a girl like me, is very important. There are tremendous changes under foot. I used to complain that my family of origin were neglectful of me, and yet my new family is obsessed with me. Both my boys hang off me daily. The rest of my time is spent making sure my son is on solid ground and then going forward into the fray.

I'm ready to step up into a better life for me and my boys. Today I can concentrate on other, better, healthier things. I'm excited about Ireland; there is a different life emerging here. There are so many lovely things about Dublin: the friends I have, the sea, the closeness to the city centre. It reminds me of Liverpool. Waking up in my own house is lovely, I have to say, and I love it here. It was vital that I settled closer to home, I needed to complete the circle. I needed to see where I stood with my family and to see what God had for me. I needed to leave and cleave; leave my old life and start a new one.

My boy is healthy, funny and strong, and I can't imagine life without him. All the love I was looking for in other places radiates from that little being. He wants me over anything else and is always so excited to see me, so it's time for me to do right by him. He's a glorious little boy and is easy enough to deal with. I'm happy that he is a good eater and sleeper; I don't know how I would have managed with a child that was harder work.

So I'm committed to standing in the grace of God rather than constantly running. God is so wonderful. I have been able to turn from the past and choose to change the direction of my life simply to protect my son. I couldn't fully do it for myself but for him I can. The chain of unpleasantness stops right here; it's time to start healing from the past and to look to the future.

Chapter Twenty-One: Give Him thanks

I am still essentially the same girl but I have shed so many skins. I want to say like a snake, but it sets me up for too many puns. Let's see: I was brought up in a household where a child had fallen into the fire; a family that would be ripped apart by divorce. I was an insecure, racially abused child; an unwanted sibling, a bullied sister.

But I have also been a child gymnast, a model, an actress, a director, a writer and a beloved daughter of the most high God. Then, after all of the Lord's redemptive work, I could add cherished wife and grateful mother to the list. The prevailing sense I am left with is one of gratitude. That I have been able to do any of the things that I dreamed about is a miracle. And that I have been able to have a wonderful family, and that we are all healthy, is just as great a miracle.

I thank God everyday for my selfless pastor Regina. She taught me what it was to be a woman and to respect myself; to save myself sexually for marriage. Most importantly, she encouraged me to distance myself from my family of origin if they had hurt me and said that God would bring new people into my life who would love me. She was right.

I thank God for Roxanna. She taught me the Word of God, as well as being fabulous, stylish and on top of her game. She jetted around the world, but still had a wonderful sense of family. I watched her with wonder as she nursed her father to the end. She's an exemplary woman.

I also watched her win the fight against breast cancer by the power of the Word of God; she is such an inspiration to me. She passed on recently, and it threw me into a sense of sadness that was debilitating, but I know she would want me to live on for my son and husband. I can't thank her enough for what she did in my life, the only thing I can think of is to pass on the learning to another woman. I'll start with my new sister Jody and let it grew from there, each one reaching one, and see where we end up.

I want to thank the girls that have walked alongside me in my life I definitely could not have made it through the muck and the mire without you. Jody is my new baby sister; we met in LA and speak daily. She is hilarious. I listen to her, pray with and guide her as best I can, as others did for me. She is another person that comes and finds me wherever I am and I am grateful to her for that. We also have a similar story with our families, so we pray for them together. And we talk a whole lot of nonsense about her quest for love. She rocks! She has a phenomenal story, an incredible attitude and, when she is ready, she will tell all.

Vera is my London-based sister in Christ and the godmother of my son. She's an excellent woman. She works in the hospital as a midwife, in the church with the youth and on the worship team as a singer and worship leader; she's like an angel. She sang at my wedding and has blessed me so often with words, prayer and little acts of kindness, especially when I was all over the TV but had very little money coming in. She has offered so much support and sistership. She inspires me to be better, to try and live better, and she is the kindest girl, neighbour and friend a woman could have.

Francina, as I call her, is my big sister. She is always there and always ready to get my back. She actually gave me my first film break as an extra in some film she was producing before I was even a model. I have known her since then, although I lost touch with her during my time away. As soon I came back I went to her house and she was packing to move out of London. If I had left it a little later, I would have lost her. We acted like not a day had passed since the last time we were together: that's the mark of a great friendship.

I got reacquainted with her as I helped her move. She came to Australia with me when I went into the jungle and was the one that met me on the famous I'm a Celebrity bridge afterwards. I knew I could trust her to have my best interests at heart when I was weak and freaked out. She also came to Dublin after I had the baby to assist, love and support me. She's an incredible girl, and is my son's other godmother. She is also very truthful with me, and can dish out tough love as well. I am blessed to have each of these wonderful, faithful ladies in my life. As I write this I understand now more than ever how hard my mother's life must have been. I have one child, she has four. I am not in my country of birth, but I'm still speaking my native English language, and I'm only across the Irish Sea. I have a fulfilling career that has been paused by motherhood and am blessed to be raising my gorgeous son with my gorgeous husband.

My mum was alone during her mid-20s and in a foreign country at a time when divorce, broken families and Nigerian women, for that matter, were not the norm. So although everything I have said is true, I still have a profound respect, empathy and love for her despite it all. She is a courageous soul and I would never have wanted anyone else to raise me.

Epilogue

Out of the blue I got a phone call asking me to come for an audition in Liverpool a few weeks later. February had been a mad time as I was deeply wounded that Roxanna had passed away. I had internalised it and was hospitalised with suspected appendicitis. Then, when leaving the hospital for a routine check-up at the doctor's I had fallen down the stairs and severely sprained my ankle. I wasn't in the mood or in good form to go and read for Hollyoaks, and my finances were battered from the sudden expense of running back from Los Angeles; so much so that I hadn't been able to get to Roxanna's funeral. I was completely disgusted at myself by that, but as we both believed she was with the Lord, I feel she would have approved of my choice to stay with my son and minister to the living. Her last words to me were "look after your son". It was still hard though.

You can't expect your agent to work for you if you suddenly want to bow out of the game when adversity strikes. So more for my relationship with Emma than anything else I decided to go. Although I have an abundance of family in Liverpool, I booked myself into the hotel I had got married in for concentration's sake. I had to ask Paolo if I could borrow money from his bank account. The exchange went like this: "Paolo, can mummy have a loan from your bank account?" Paolo looked at me very sweetly and said "no". I tried again. He wasn't even two, so perhaps he didn't understand the importance of it. "Oh go on Pao, mummy has an audition that's very important...Peees?" That's the way he said please!

He blanked me. So I decided to override him and take the money, which was largely the money I had saved for him anyway. But I remember mum taking my savings when I was a kid so I was annoyed with myself that I was doing the same thing and vowed to pay him back. So now the pressure was on: I had literally robbed my child's piggy bank! How low can you go?

From start to finish the whole episode was amusing. I decided it was time to rid myself of all the fake hair. I had cut my hair off months earlier in sympathy when Roxanna was going through chemo. It looked a bit crazy, but I was in a belligerent mood. I decided I was fed up with the fake nails and had recently got my body back in shape without all the surgery I had fantasised about. So I decided to go in as me, simple plain ole me. The flight attendant on the plane said: "Didn't you used to work on TV?" Oh, my ego was on the ropes! I explained to her that I still did and was actually going for an audition in Liverpool and she explained to her younger colleague that I was once a TV star! She wished me good luck and said she had loved Footballers' Wives.

When I got there, the first thing I noticed on the premises was a tiny cute nursery. Obviously that is really important for me now. My priorities have shifted and I had been praying that my son and I would be together and that he would have a safe, educationally sound nursery while I worked in TV. I chuckled when I saw this because I know only God can sort these things!

A man was saying goodbye to someone outside and putting them in a taxi. When he came in I started taking the mickey, pretending to cry, doing all that boo hoo drama… He took it in good humour. I went to the desk to sign in, but when I said my name the receptionist looked at me blankly as it wasn't on the list. She checked thoroughly through the pages but it was nowhere to be seen. That type of thing can really unnerve you, but I decided to pick my chin up off the floor and get on with preparing for the part.

I met one the directors and he said: "Did you know Paul from Footballers' Wives? Love your hair…Ohhh, we've never had that look here". I saw he was with the man I had taken the mickey out of earlier. It turns out the guy was one of the writers! He asked if I was auditioning for the part of Gabby and explained she was "dead genuine". I thought that was very good advice because the script read as though she could have been a big-time manipulator.

One of the casting people said: "You here for Gabby? Lose the Scouse accent." In my nerves I had pumped up the remains of my own accent to ridiculous proportions because I figured I was in Liverpool so I wanted them to know I was a proud card-carrying member of the Scouse squadron. I finally went into the waiting room for the casting. There was an actress there who looked like the character I had created for Footballers' Wives. She was a dark-skinned black girl in jeans and high-heeled boots with a weave down to her waist.

There was also a medium, light-skinned actress in jeans with a nice bobbed haircut, a very light-skinned girl with really short hair in jeans, a statuesque blond in jeans, an Italian-looking brunette in jeans and a lovely looking tomboyish woman in jeans and a plaid shirt. To say they had cast the net wide was an understatement, but everyone had gone for the 'mothers wear jeans' bit. There I was with my cleavage out in a skintight, flowery dress. I looked a bit country and western with fishnet tights and ankle boots over my damaged ankle. I was so different from the other actresses. My experience told me I had either got it right or I'd got it really, really wrong. I was about fifth to go in and the previous four came in and out a bit too fast for my liking. So I decided that when I went in I was going slow things down a little. I certainly did that!

After I was done with my audition I went back to Dublin. The following day they asked me to come back to Liverpool, and this time when I got there my name was the only one on the list! I didn't understand the significance of this at the time. Then they gave me about six scenes to deal with and I snuck off into a room to learn them.

Then I popped out to go to the toilet and ran into one of the regulars who was looking for me. Apparently he had come to help me! How amazing is that?! I have never been on a show where an established actor would be bothered to do that! So we had the luxury of working together for half an hour, whoa. I went in and was told I was there to be matched with him (the Hollyoaks regular) and my prospective screen kids! An hour later I had the part and was looking for a house for me and my family in Liverpool. I even paid Paolo back so his bank balance has been restored!

Jesus!

The disaster at Hollyoaks was instantaneous; it started on the very first day. When I got there, having carefully studying my lines, I realised they had rewritten the opening scene. In truth they had only added a couple of lines, but it was enough to unnerve me. On the one hand they do an incredible job of organising four blocks at the same time – that's four crews and hundreds of actors, personnel and crew members – but on the other, there was absolute chaos in the passing on of information, especially the rewriting of scripts.

Nick Pickard who has played Tony since the first ever episode told me they would hire me for a year, which they didn't. They hired our little black family for six months, but the other two white families that came right behind us were hired for the year. I had to pretend I didn't know, but I couldn't help myself as one of those actresses was with my agent. I asked her to inquire and she came back with the disquieting news that "they weren't quite sure about our family". It wasn't a great start.

There were plenty of signs of trouble at the mill to be honest. Lydia Lloyd Henry, who played my daughter, was a very mature looking fourteen-year-old. She was absolutely gorgeous, but she was supposed to be playing a twelve-year-old and actually looked twenty-one. She had a lot of studying to do as she was in a critical year at school. Added to this, she lived in Manchester and had no acting experience or training for the job. I really liked her a lot, but I was worried about these things.

Shaun Blackstock was also a new actor, but at eighteen he had nearly completed his dramatic training. As he lived around the corner from me, I took him under my wing and we often worked very hard together at night preparing scenes. He blossomed, but they didn't given him much to do, which was a real shame.

I, on the other hand, worked every single day, which I loved. The only drawback was that my two-year-old Paolo was two and was spending twelve hours in nursery while I was on set. When I finally got him home, I basically fed him, bathed him and tried to get him to go to sleep so that I could do it all again the next day. Stefano was still living in Dublin, where his permanent position was, so Hollyoaks split my family. Or another way of looking at it is that I split my family by taking the job. Either way, it was a bittersweet experience.

I was delighted to be home and delighted to be working, but I was really under the gun. The Hollyoaks executives kept doing these big advertising campaigns where they would cherry pick new cast members. They always used the two white families and old favourites like the McQueens, whom I love! Even more perplexing, though, was that the executive producer, Paul Marquess, worked me very hard; so hard that other actors started to question how much I was earning and how many episodes I was in. I was smart enough not to answer these questions; I just got my head down and carried on with the job in hand.

Producers started coming to our sets to watch Lydia and Shaun. Lydia, especially, kept getting dragged in for extra acting lessons from the set coach. There were complaints that she held up production because she was either unprepared or unbelievable. I don't recall that, but this was a lot of pressure for a young actress. The final straw came when she and another young actor had a storyline in which she was supposed to be pregnant. Apparently, the episode was taken to London to show the Channel 4 people and it fell flat. Luckily, I wasn't in that scene; however, I heard there was stifled laughter when it was shown.

We had re-signed our contracts for a further six months and then one day when I was walking down the driveway of Lime Pictures I saw a whole bunch of young black male actors coming out of casting. They were too young to be my love interests and too old to be my son, so I immediately knew something was about to drop. This was my twenty-sixth TV show so I know the game backwards. Generally speaking, you don't get more than one black character or family at any one time on a mainstream UK show, so I knew this spelt trouble. Also, I had been called in to do some publicity for the next episode and by the time I responded (quickly, I might add), the publicist said: "Oh, don't worry about it!"

The last clue was that I was doing a 10k with some other former cast members, and my name was also listed as a former cast member. I knew this wasn't a mistake. Plenty of Hollyoaks actors had found out they were off the job through crew members or carelessness. So one day I was sitting in makeup making some wig choices to try and move the character along, when I was called up to Paul Marquess's office. As I crossed the threshold, he said: "It's not good news." He then proceeded to talk. I didn't really hear him, but the gist of it was that we were being given a break for six months and might come back, but then again we might not. "We were going to go and visit my sick father"... well all's I can say is he must be really sick because after we shot that rapid exit scene, we never returned.

I was personally humiliated; there's nothing worse than losing your job. I was embarrassed and slow to grasp what was being said, but I thanked him for my time there. I went back to makeup and made my excuses and got on the train to London as I was appearing on The Wright Stuff the next day. The phone started ringing immediately: Lydia was crying, Shaun was swearing and other actors were asking if I was ok.

The hardest part for me was uprooting Paolo again. So for the following four months I drove him to that set, left my ego at the gate and withstood all the phoney nonsense because I wanted him to have some continuity. I made the difficult decision to stay in Liverpool even though my husband was in Dublin. In Liverpool I have a new girl gang forming, Bukky, Maxine, Shirley, Christabell, Desiree, Dominque, Elaine and Miss Gee, I salute them all, their help faith and encouragement got me through a really tough time

The survivor in me kicked in, I realized its hard to hit a moving target so though I really wanted to have a long term pity party, I cut my loses with Hollyoaks, and I very quickly got a presenting job on BBC Radio Merseyside show Upfront and began to write a column for the Liverpool Echo, which I had to beg them for and I did it mostly unpaid. I needed to prove to myself that I wasn't all washed up, and to my husband that I had good reason to stay in Liverpool. It was a tough time as I immediately isolated myself from the cast, even though I lived next door to Bronagh Waugh who played Cheryl. I just couldn't bear to hear about the functions and the days on set. I had struggled to make friends there, not because the cast were unfriendly, but simply because I couldn't go out every night. I had a two year old boy to care for at home as I learned my lines for the next day every night, that had to be my priority.

I was shooting every day and sometimes when I did agree to go I had to back out in order to be mum. I didn't have a reliable system for his care at this point, and frankly I didn't have the heart to be parading around Liverpool with people I was at least a decade older than, even though they were all quite lovely. More importantly, I watched how quickly their former colleagues were uninvited to parties after they had worked with them for years.

I hadn't strengthened any bonds with the cast like I could have; it simply wasn't the right season. I wish I could have spent more time with them, but there just weren't enough hours in the day. The disappointment with Hollyoaks could have killed me, but I knew that I had to mourn it quick and then move on.

When I told the PR people I was forty they nearly had a nervous breakdown. It was only three years older than the lie that had been circulated, but I didn't want to live in my home town having to lie and hide. I will never regret that. I was the same age as the executives not the cast for the most part.

I couldn't have predicted becoming a columnist for the Echo or a presenter on Upfront. But running my mouth for a living in both posts, it has restored my links within the community I hadn't lived in for twenty-five years. Paolo and I settled and found a home after reshuffling a few plans. We were also blessed that Stefano was able to get a post in Salford, so we were all able to live together. Needless to say, I love Liverpool and I love life, so I'm eager to see what the next season brings.

There is a wonderful sense of accomplishment that comes when you survive the fire, or are born into the flames of struggle. What twist and turns my life has taken! I can honestly say I have done some very exciting things; things that if you had seen me at four or fourteen you wouldn't have believed could be done.

So, bruised one, wherever you are don't give up, don't give in. There is a wonderful plan and destiny for your life. If you don't trust me when I tell you this, listen to that small gentle voice in your spirit: it's the spirit of God.

*The Spirit of the Lord God is upon me
Because the Lord has anointed me
To preach good tidings to the poor;
He has sent me to heal the broken-hearted,
To proclaim liberty to the captives,
And the opening of the prison to those who are bound;
To proclaim the acceptable year of the Lord,
And the day of vengeance of our God;
To comfort all who mourn,
To console those who mourn in Zion,
To give them beauty for ashes,
The oil of joy for mourning*

Isaiah 61:1-3